Praise for *Everything We Know About Leadership*

"Right now, we need stories of courageous leadership—and the guidance they offer—more than ever. The powerful lessons in this work can help each of us build our strengths. Thank you!"

Frances Moore Lappé | Small Planet Institute

"Many of us find it difficult to move out of our silos, if we even think of doing it at all. This book explores ALF's unique process for helping leaders understand how to bridge divides, create new networks of unusual allies and help generate new thinking around system stalemates."

C.S. Park | Director, Seagate Technology

"I participated in ALF soon after being elected to the Houston City Council, but after years of work as a community activist and experience heading many non-profit groups. My experience helped me communicate and work toward goals in new ways. The close bonds I was able to forge with a diverse array of leaders affected how I understand the world and how I continue to act today. The network of those with the shared ALF bond has been a resource in tackling tough problems.

Everything We Know About Leadership serves to remind readers of one of the most important lessons I have learned: a true leader has agreed to accept the challenge of leading. Too often what we call leadership is following from the front."

Annise Parker | Mayor, Houston, Texas

"The ALF leadership experience is unlike any other. There is a deep and sophisticated understanding of the tough challenges we face today, and ALF offers the time, creates the space, and gives the tools and guidance needed for leaders to become not simply powerful, but transformative. This book reveals and explains the foundational elements that created this unique and dynamic program."

Dr. Greg Papadopoulos | Sun Microsystems - Former CTO

"*Everything We Know About Leadership* is a remarkable and inspiring chronicle about leaders coming together in amazingly creative and value-driven ways, across every divide imaginable, to serve the common good. It is also an inviting cookbook that is applicable for leaders anywhere wanting to explore a different style and substance of leadership whether in high school, college, graduate school, or any venue. It makes clear how small groups working collaboratively can not only be exponentially more effective than old school forms, but can also find beneficial and generous solutions that no traditional leader can. This beautifully written book stands out as a great contribution to the field."

John Steiner | Founding Member, Transpartisan Center

"This book distills for me what I have learned about leadership through ALF (or have forgotten). That it will extend and enrich through an ongoing future dialogue what hundreds throughout the country have learned from their ALF experience is very exciting."

Jack Peterson | President, Bellarmine Preparatory School

"There is no better laboratory of leadership than the 30 years of work that the American Leadership Forum has undertaken. The impact on the thousands of community leaders who have engaged in this systematic, thoughtful and profound experience of servant leadership is immeasurable. The writing of this book is a natural evolution of the ALF community engaging leaders for the purpose of developing a more robust and socially responsible community of leadership that will start, attempt, undertake and initiate the next great evolution of our communities."

Joe Lawless | Executive Director, Center for Leadership & Social Responsibility, Milgard School of Business, University of Washington Tacoma

"*Everything We Know About Leadership* is inspiring, textured, and authentic. It gives the reader a lived sense of how the tension of difference fuels growth in leaders, how true dialogue is forged in contemplation, and how the historical context surrounding the founding of the American Leadership Forum seeded the launch of class after class of participants. Anyone interested in renewing their experience as a leader, those ready to put an end to the isolation that can come with achievement, and people primed for substantive hope of what 'we' can accomplish will find themselves in this book."

Leticia Nieto, Psy.D. | Author, Beyond Inclusion, Beyond Empowerment: A Developmental Strategy to Liberate Everyone

"*Everything We Know About Leadership* is an expression of ALF's promise to 'strengthen capacities for community change.' The book provides a honest review of what we know, what we think we know, and what we need to know about leadership interconnectedness. ALF isn't afraid to test its value. Each Senior Fellow strives to provoke change and be accountable for their community. It's only natural for ALF to turn inward and expect these things from its organizational self."

Julie Anderson | Auditor, Pierce County, Washington

"*Everything We Know About Leadership* and the American Leadership Forum do not present us with a new leadership philosophy or prescription. Instead, they bring us to the center of what we intuitively know it takes to bring about transformational change in our communities. Through personal testimonials and ground-truthed examples, we are reminded that leadership is an exhilarating and humbling practice that calls on its practitioners to deepen knowledge of self, embrace and harness the potency of diversity and remain fearless and inspiring servants of the common good. And maybe most importantly, that cultivating these strengths within a community of likeminded pilgrims might be the essential and highest calling after all."

Brian Boyd | Executive Director, Forest and Sequoia Foundations

"*Everything We Know About Leadership* tells the story of ALF and reminds me of the importance of dialogue and collaboration. It also makes me realize that changing the world for the better requires both."

Alex Bunin | Public Defender, Harris County, Texas

"Successful leadership in our ever changing world requires cultivated team building among mutually respectful participants inspired to work together in an open and inviting environment towards common goals. They epitomize a dedicated commitment to address problems and seize opportunities by sharing experiences, knowledge and innovative ideas through dialog, collaboration and consensus building, all in accordance with the tenets of ALF."

Ed Wulfe | CEO, Wulfe & Co

EVERYTHING
WE KNOW ABOUT
LEADERSHIP
IS LESS THAN WE
STILL HAVE TO LEARN

Jeff Golden

IN DIALOGUE WITH

The American Leadership Forum,
Sharon Babcock, Chris Block,
Kent Snyder, Robin Teater, Anne Udall

Everything We Know About Leadership
Is Less Than We Still Have To Learn

By Jeff Golden
in Dialogue with
The American Leadership Forum,
Sharon Babcock, Chris Block, Kent Snyder,
Robin Teater, Anne Udall

American Leadership Forum
3101 Richmond Avenue, Suite 140
Houston, TX 77098
www.alfnational.org
www.everythingweknowaboutleadership.org

Book design by Mary Holste
Printed in the United States

To those serving their communities in so many ways and so many places, enriching both the future and their own lives through their deepening connection with one another.

"Water is fluid, soft, and yielding. But water will wear away rock, which is rigid and cannot yield. As a rule, whatever is fluid, soft, and yielding will overcome whatever is rigid and hard. This is another paradox: what is soft is strong."

—Lao-Tzu (600 B.C.)

TABLE OF CONTENTS

FOREWORD

By Peter Block

E<small>VERYTHING</small> W<small>E</small> K<small>NOW</small> A<small>BOUT</small> L<small>EADERSHIP</small> presents the story of an inspired and successful leadership training effort by the American Leadership Forum. ALF was created to bring to the world a more conscious, transparent, and collaborative form of leadership. It began by bringing together a diverse group of leaders in Houston and providing them a learning experience destined to change their lives, especially their lives together. The book narrates the nature of the experience, the good it has done, and how it has spread around the country. This is in itself a good story, but the story opens the possibility of something larger.

The something larger is about caring for the common good. What I appreciate about the ALF approach is its intentional focus on bringing compassion and care to the whole community—all citizens and all institutions. There is a great need for leadership that cares for the commons, especially in our modern market-minded culture that is mostly driven by self-interest, competition, and fierce ideology.

The care for the common good evident in the ALF approach stands in contrast to much of our leadership development that is still based on a heroic model—leader as great individual, leader as self-made visionary, role model, a big star. ALF's boldness is to advocate a kind of leadership that is not a child of our materialistic and dependency-loving culture. Instead the intent is to create an alternative leadership model organized around altruism, interdependence, and receptivity. ALF creates learning conditions in which leaders are encouraged to welcome strangers rather than reinforce the like-mindedness that holds the stranger as an "other."

This is not the leadership that modern culture is particularly looking for; it is more the leadership the culture is waiting for. We need more leadership that restores our humanity. ALF does not just imagine or dream of this kind of leadership; it has created the lived experience for thousands of people. This book makes concrete and explicit what leadership based on collaboration in service of the common good looks like, tastes like, and feels like.

The learning methodology described in this reporting is as important as its lofty purpose and the anecdotal testimony of the results that have come out of it. This story is reconstructing both the intent of leadership and the teaching of leadership. Here is how:

With every activity structured around interdependence, leadership becomes all about relationships. It means that relationships take priority over results, or role modeling, or pitching a vision that others can enroll in. It declares that relationships are primary and central to performance and to learning. This also means that the most important relationships are among peers. The traditional culture declares that leadership is about the connection between leaders and followers. A culture that cares for the common good declares that leadership occurs among equals.

The ALF approach is a curriculum whose primary purpose is to reconnect participants with their humanness, and with the Earth. It evokes the journey inward, connecting people to themselves and the realization that what they have is enough, that what they are is enough. This is the antidote to the "not-enoughness" of our current fast-paced, more is better society.

ALF confronts the myth of self-sufficiency, the autonomous man or woman. Its organizing principle is that we are absolutely dependent on each other. Not one of us has made it on our own. There is no endeavor—not art, not science, not one business in the world—that has made it without a support system. None of us is successful without other people making sacrifices so that we can succeed. Even Robinson Crusoe, the epitome of someone alone, stranded on an island, needed a support system to keep from going mad. The design for interdependence is a decisive element of every learning experience. It trumps content and information every time. This is the methodology of restoration.

There are other aspects of the ALF effort that have big implications. Each group has a service project that keeps people in touch with each other. This is much needed, for we live in a transitory society. Agility, flexibility, letting go, embracing change are elements of the contemporary mantra. We learn to make close friends quickly and move on at the same speed. ALF seeks stability. It supports localization. It brings local leadership teams together over time. It gives the teams something useful to do; sometimes the doing has to do with their hands, an undertaking very different from working in the virtual world, which is pure abstraction. To know that we are in this together, in this place, over time, changes the world.

What ALF is creating is a liturgy for transformation. Liturgy is the order of the service, the order of the process of inviting mystery and all that is sacred into our community and thereby into our lives. One example of the liturgy in this effort is the ritual of the seven minute talk. No need to explain it here; you will find it later in the book. For now it is enough to say that it is a simple form for each to declare a purpose and a future. This seven minute talk is just one little structure in the ALF approach. All the other structures you will read about—the details of choosing to participate, of preparation, of arrival, of journey, of speaking, of aloneness and collaboration—are the elements that integrate leadership with learning.

The dominant culture associates leadership with knowing. It desperately seeks leadership that demonstrates control and promises predictability. ALF is creating an alternative. What we historically value, in Lincoln, in Gandhi, in Christ, Buddha, and Mohammed, is leadership that can care for the commons, that can listen to those on the margin, that can imagine a future really distinct from the present. It is a prophetic leadership of not knowing, a leadership of surprise, and relatedness, and mystery. What will be restorative to our communities is a leadership of intimate relatedness and an openness to surprise. This is the point of this book: beyond the elegant spirit of its beginning, beyond the travelogue of its journey, it invites a use of legitimate power that heals our separation, lifts our intentions, and values and acts on the well-being of the whole.

As a final commentary, reading *Everything We Know About Leadership* opens the possibility that under the right conditions, the current leadership of our communities may have the capacity to transform some basic tenets of our modern society: the tenets of autonomy, individualism, and competition.

The alternative to a "what about me?" world is a citizen world. This is the premise of democracy, a way of living together where citizens know that what is needed does not have to be purchased, but can be cooperatively created. They decide to move their attention away from the mall and back to the neighborhood. This calls for the kind of leadership that brings citizens together, that values listening over speaking, cooperation over winning, the quality of living over the quantity of living. This is what it will take for us to really care for the common good. This is what building community is really about: an end to entitlement, a willingness to yield some on individual rights, to undo some of our longing for privacy and privatization. Even a willingness to learn to be happy with less, realizing that our children will be better off than we are; their houses will just be smaller.

This is a big step, almost beyond our imagination, but the work of the American Leadership Forum is lighting the way, proving in its work and through this book that it is surely possible. Knowing that leadership for the common good is happening in a few cities, with a few groups of leaders, opens a path for us all.

Peter Block
December 2012

INTRODUCTION

THIS IS A STORY of relentless hope, occasional disappointment, hard-earned discoveries and wonderful achievements. It doesn't have a happy ending, because it doesn't have an ending at all.

It begins with an experience shared by some four thousand men and women across America. Many of them will tell you that it has enriched their lives, and indirectly the lives of people around them, in lasting ways. These people have invested generous portions of time, passion, and energy toward the common good of their communities.

> "Do all that you can, with what you have, in that time that you have, in the place you are."
>
> —Nkosi Johnson, South African AIDS activist who lived to twelve years of age

This is not what distinguishes them. Millions of people in thousands of places care about and give to their communities. What distinguishes the members of this group is that their service has been vitally amplified by the year each of them spent in the American Leadership Forum.

This book tells the story of ALF, describing its origins, the web of values in which it does its work and the elements of the program designed to advance those values. We will get a sense of the impact that ALF has on the lives and work of its *senior fellows*—the men and women who've completed the one- to two-year ALF experience—and, more to the point, on the communities where they live and work. This book also builds the platform for an ongoing exploration—an inquiry that by its essential nature has no end—of pressing challenges facing all communities, and the people who want to serve them, in years ahead.

ALF senior fellows are people who've shown commitment and proficiency in working for their communities, and who learn and adapt in the process. What they are not are people who think they have a corner on the secrets to great leadership and civic engagement. If anyone ventures to tell you categorically what leadership is and is not, or offers a guaranteed recipe

> "The world suffers much more today from unquestioned answers than from unanswered questions."
>
> —participant in a Peter Senge workshop

for community improvement, you can be fairly sure that you're not talking to someone from the ALF community. An ALF senior fellow would be more likely to say that most popular assumptions about leadership have been clear, instructive and—recent history suggests—wrong, or at least seriously incomplete.

OUT OF WATERGATE

In the course of recent history, the formative event for ALF was the monument of failed leadership that came to be known as Watergate. A young Houston lawyer named Joseph Jaworski knew its grim particulars before almost anyone else. His father, Leon Jaworski, was the special prosecutor who helped uncover the web of crime and abuses, and he confided deeply in Joe along the way. In his 1996 book, *Synchronicity*, Joseph describes his initial reaction to the incriminating White House tapes:

> His [Richard Nixon's] betrayal of the Constitution and his staggering abuse of power made me sick to my stomach. Revulsion and hate welled up in me. I had a feeling of fear for our entire country, fear that followed the realization that we were being led by a man with so little character. How could someone with such a low moral and ethical base ascend to the highest office of the most powerful nation in the world? How could this happen?

Jaworski's hunger for answers ignited a long and consequential personal voyage. He remembered his earliest impressions of leadership, back when his father belonged to what Joe later called the "8F Club." Suite 8F of the sixteen-story Lamar Hotel, which dominated downtown Houston's skyline through Joe's boyhood, was the setting for a quiet lunch every Friday. It was not an especially elegant setting. Richard Connelly described it in "Houston 101: Where Kingmakers Reigned and Plotted," a 2009 posting on *HoustonPress.com*:

> The suite had only two rooms and a kitchenette and it was decorated in whatever the relevant time period's definition of "tacky" was, but it became the Unofficial Capital of Texas. George R. Brown of Brown & Root was the nominal host, but the guest list included people like Jesse Jones, owner of the *Chronicle*, William Hobby, owner of the *Post*, Clint Murchison, LBJ and John Connally... From 8F Johnson's political career was financed—Robert Caro's epic biography of the 36th President is full of tales of Connally hauling suitcases of cash to and from the room. And, just as importantly to those present, the Oil Depletion Allowance was savagely protected. The allowance was an utter giveaway to oil barons; it let them declare 27.5 percent of their income to be tax-free.
>
> It's not difficult to imagine the scene—cigars, bourbon, some eye-candy to help serve—and a rabid hatred for the New Deal and anything that threatened the oil bidness [sic]. If publicity was needed on an issue, the *Chronicle* and *Post* were there to serve. Governors, senators, congressmen all trooped in—some hat-in-hand; others, like LBJ, part of the team. (Johnson was able to bash the New Deal in 8F and praise it to the skies on the stump. He was just that kinda guy.)
>
> Huge federal contracts for shipyards, for dams, for highways, all were parceled out in 8F. Careers were broken if the person in question got in the way; who knows how many livelihoods were crushed by a simple nod of the head by someone in 8F?

That's how things worked, in many more cities than Houston and more states than Texas, for a long time. And it worked partly because beyond serving their own interests, these privileged men cared about serving the interests, as they saw them, of their communities. They were civic fathers who cared about their offspring.

Today there's a stark concrete parking garage where the Lamar Hotel stood and Suite 8F sounds like a relic from feudal times. The political and social insurrection of the 1960s pushed crony-style hierarchical leadership underground, until the unlikely circumstances of Watergate brought it back to the surface and lasting disgrace.

Joseph Jaworski harnessed his disillusionment in service to a deep personal commitment. His goal was nothing less than a transformation in the nature and practice of leadership in our society. His chosen vehicle, carefully designed in collaboration with extraordinary thinkers whose journeys resembled his own, would be the American Leadership Forum.

As these words are written, we mark the thirtieth anniversary of the very first ALF class. And the layered economic, political and social crises of the 21st century's opening years bring forward the same question about institutional leadership that Jaworski asked three decades ago: *How could this happen?* For many of us, the question is not an academic proposition, but the seed of a renewed commitment to service in uncertain and sometimes bewildering times.

NOWHERE NEAR SUITE 8F

For the most part, our moment in history is clearly different from the sobering aftermath of Watergate. We don't start, as Jaworski and his colleagues did, in the shadows of unapologetic hierarchical leadership. We're not standing outside the door of Suite 8F anymore, and most people understand leadership, citizenship, and organizational relationships in much different ways than did those unchallenged cigar-smoking leaders. The American Leadership Forum has played a role in this change, and has more to offer.

This book illuminates that role—the past contributions, the work under way, the insights gained and ongoing efforts to deepen service to our communities. Part I, *Leadership Defined*, briefly recounts ALF's history and the principles and theory of change that shaped its design. In Part II, *Leadership Applied*, we look at ALF's five core values—primacy of relationship; appreciation, exploration, and inclusion of diversity; dialogue and collaboration; service to the common good; inner reflection and personal growth—and how they have played out for some senior fellows in the matrix of complexities that make up everyday life. Part III, *Leadership Evolving*, looks forward. We identify and summarize some of the ongoing challenges that face anyone dedicated to advancing the common good. Here's where we face up to a serious limitation of traditional leadership books. The pace of change in civic, social, and organizational life can begin to erode the relevance of bound material immediately after the last word is written. With that in mind, and staunchly embracing ALF's belief in the foundational importance of collaborative intelligence, we will close the book by inviting you into an ongoing dialogue on insights, experiences and observations about leadership and its adaptation to a world that will not stop changing. You will find that dialogue at www.everythingweknowaboutleadership.org.

We invite you to join us in ALF's continuing venture to expand this evolving form of leadership—the kind of leadership that will continue to reveal new insights and possibilities throughout our communities and the world.

PART I

LEADERSHIP DEFINED:
ALF'S ROOTS, THEORY AND PRACTICE

CHAPTER 1:
THE FOUNDING OF THE
AMERICAN LEADERSHIP FORUM

IT WAS A LONG JOURNEY, tenacious and intense, driven by a profoundly personal quest.

Without knowing the methods or means, Joseph Jaworski, stunned by what his father uncovered as the Watergate Special Prosecutor, committed himself to transforming the nature of leadership in our nation. Joseph's journey, chronicled years later in *Synchronicity: The Inner Path of Leadership*, upended his personal life, his career track, and his core beliefs. Following his deepest instincts, Jaworski sought out individuals who had thought with unusual clarity about human interaction and the phenomenon of leadership. He absorbed—even if he didn't immediately understand—an extraordinary range of ideas, hypotheses, and unfolding mental constructs.

His access to individuals who normally welcomed very little engagement probably had something to do with his fiercely tenacious curiosity. "I've never met anybody," wrote his friend and colleague Peter Senge in the introduction to *Synchronicity*, "who's as good at wondering as Joe is."

ENCOUNTERS WITH GREENLEAF, HESSE AND BOHM
Jaworski's learning encounters would have defining impacts on what was to follow, especially reading the writings of Robert

Greenleaf, Hermann Hesse and talking with Dr. David Bohm.

In *Synchronicity*, Jaworski writes of finding in his mail one day an unsolicited copy of *The Servant as Leader*, a slim pamphlet by Robert Greenleaf:

> The moment I saw the words Servant as Leader, they had an enormous impact on me. The very notion of servant leadership was absolutely stunning to me, and I couldn't put it out of my mind. It was as if someone had suddenly cleansed my lens of perception, enabling me to understand what I had been struggling with for so long; at the same time, it was as if a memory of long ago had been reawakened.

In *The Servant as Leader*, Greenleaf describes how he took inspiration for his work from Hermann Hesse's *Journey to the East*:

> In this story we see a band of men on a mythical journey, probably also Hesse's own journey. The central figure of the story is Leo, who accompanies the party as the servant who does their menial chores, but who also sustains them with his spirit and his song. He is a person of extraordinary presence. All goes well until Leo disappears. Then the group falls into disarray and the journey is abandoned. They cannot make it without the servant Leo. The narrator, one of the party, after some years of wandering finds Leo and is taken into the Order that had sponsored the journey. There he discovers that Leo, whom he had known first as servant, was in fact the titular head of the Order, its guiding spirit, a great and noble leader.

David Bohm, a groundbreaking theoretical physicist and close associate of Albert Einstein, may have had an even more consequential impact on Jaworski's thinking. Bohm's work, which

> "There is too much intellectual wheel spinning, too much retreating into 'research,' too little preparation for and willingness to undertake the hard and high risk tasks of building better institutions in an imperfect world, too little disposition to see 'the problem' as residing in here and not out there."
>
> —**Robert Greenleaf,**
> ***The Servant as Leader***

wove together emerging understanding of the physical, social, psychological, and spiritual dimensions of the human experience, affirmed an indivisible unity of all living matter. Jaworski looked back with enormous gratitude on an afternoon they spent together near the end of Bohm's life. The older man's remarks in that single conversation, summarized later in *Synchronicity*, crystallized Jaworski's far-flung inquiry:

> Bohm had shared with me in London an explicit mental model of the way he believed the world works and the way he believed human beings learn and think. To Bohm it was clear that humans have an innate capacity for collective intelligence. They can learn and think together, and this collaborative thought can lead to coordinated action. We are all connected and operate within living fields of thought and perception. The world is not fixed but is in constant flux; accordingly, the future is not fixed, and so can be shaped. Humans possess significant tacit knowledge—we know more than we can say. The question to be resolved: how to remove the blocks and tap into that knowledge in order to create the kind of future we all want?

Bohm offered one useful answer to that question, a methodical approach to group communication he labeled *Dialogue*, which MIT/Sloan lecturer William Isaacs has called "a conversation with a center, not sides." When used in the way that Isaacs and Bohm prescribe, Dialogue

"From time to time, the tribe gathered in a circle. They just talked and talked and talked, apparently to no purpose. They made no decision. There was no leader. And everybody could participate. There may have been wise men or wise women who were listened to a bit more—the older ones—but everybody could talk. The meeting went on, until it finally seemed to stop for no reason at all and the group dispersed. Yet after that, everybody seemed to know what to do, because they understood each other so well. Then they could get together in smaller groups and do something or decide things."

—David Bohm, *On Dialogue*

can free people from preconceptions, assumptions, conditioned reactions, and unspoken psychological needs that routinely distort communication. It expands our capacity to suspend judgment about what we hear from others. Chapter 6, "Dialogue and Collaboration," describes some of the principles and the distinctively powerful effects of this practice.

Jaworski's single conversation with Bohm infused his commitment with direction and a more exhilarating sense of what was possible. Without fully understanding the path he was on, he knew it was right for him. He describes the singular power of that moment in *Synchronicity*:

> When we parted, Bohm's final words to me were, "Everything starts with you and me." As I walked away, I knew I would have to find a way for the Leadership Forum to give its fellows an "inner education" so that they would identify themselves with all humanity. If they could do that, they could literally help change the world.

DESIGNING THE PROGRAM

What initial design features would give this ambitious new venture its best chance for success? Over time and what must have been many hours of intense dialogue, Jaworski and the thought leaders he engaged began to imagine the program components that could yield leaders committed to the public good. Early in their discussions they pinpointed what they judged to be the most damaging shortcomings of prevailing leaders. Contemporary leaders, they asserted, tended to lack understanding of the nature of leadership itself and its underlying values, of the means and requirements of effecting change, and of world conditions and the interdependence of the

> *"Those who do not have power over the story that dominates their lives, the power to retell it, rethink it, deconstruct it ....and change it as times change truly are powerless because they cannot think new thoughts."*
>
> —**Salman Rushdie**

United States with the rest of the world. They failed to appreciate the relevance of stakeholders, the implications of pluralism, and the fact that nobody is "in charge," as well as the critical importance of context—the external environment of their activities. They were prone to emphasizing forces and elements that separate rather than those that foster interconnectedness. And at the very root of the matter, their level of self-knowledge and awareness seemed superficial.

The development of creative leadership, Jaworski insisted, would require three fundamental shifts of mind: a shift in the way we think about the world, a shift in our understanding of relationship and a shift in the nature of our commitment. Key to nurturing these shifts would be the adoption of *five core values*, described one-by-one in chapters four through eight, and their consistent integration into the ALF experience.

THE FIRST ALF CHAPTERS

Where would ALF's initial resources come from? Over the years, Jaworski and his father had earned the respect and trust of the Houston business community. That was the natural place to find start-up funding and a critical mass of support. The inaugural class of the American Leadership Forum gathered in Houston in early April 1983, at the Houstonian Hotel, about five miles from where the Lamar Hotel and Suite 8F had once stood.

"ALF," said Joe Synan, a former energy industry executive who took over ALF's operational reins shortly after its founding, "is something that happened at just the right time." In the wake of Watergate, aware Americans were ready to leave Suite 8F–style leadership aside. A milepost of the times was the election of Kathy Whitmire, Houston's first woman mayor, in 1981. She was also the first to defeat a candidate selected and backed by the 8F group.

ALF's second chapter soon followed, after Jaworski happened upon Denis Mullane, then CEO of Connecticut Mutual Life Insurance, during a morning run near the Houstonian Hotel. Denis casually asked Joe what he was involved with. Joe described the founding of the ALF chapter there in Houston. "We could really use something like that in Hartford," Denis replied. He convened a group of insurance company CEOs to meet Jaworski. In 1984, ALF's second chapter opened in Hartford, Connecticut.

Across the country at about the same time, a young Multnomah County, Oregon commissioner named Earl Blumenauer was preparing a speech on leadership for City Club of Portland. He wasn't happy with what he saw around him and wanted to temper his criticism with traces of hope and possibility. He was intrigued by the fresh writings of a Houston attorney and on a sudden impulse placed a telephone call to him. Joseph Jaworski picked up the phone and the conversation that followed led to the creation of ALF's Oregon chapter, the first that spanned an entire state. "It could have been a Portland chapter instead," says Blumenauer, currently a U.S. Congressman, "but if everyone is from the same pod, you're not really leading, you're not stretching. Every state has some version of a rural/urban divide, and we wanted to take on ours."

The first Oregon class was full of the state's most vital leaders. Besides Blumenauer, the class included the CEO of the state's largest utility, the first woman speaker of the state House of

> *"A nation is never finished. You can't build it and then leave it standing as Pharoahs did the pyramids. It has to be built and rebuilt, recreated in each generation by believing, caring men and women. It is now our turn. If we don't believe and don't care, nothing can save the nation. If we believe and care, nothing can stop us."*
>
> **—John Gardner**

Representatives, the head of the state's preeminent business association and the head of the Bonneville Power Administration. "We were going to do more than just raise a few dollars and set the thing up," Blumenauer says. "We picked people who had real jobs, too many commitments, and no time."

Next came California's Silicon Valley, which hummed with a daring entrepreneurial ambition that seemed fertile to Jaworski.

The founding effort there tapped into the support and guidance of John Gardner, probably America's most widely respected authority at the time on quality leadership.

Gardner's view was that no place needed ALF more than the Silicon Valley. He found an able collaborator in civic leader Ann Debusk, who played the primary role in establishing the Silicon Valley chapter.

Several of the young high-tech industry's most dynamic leaders stepped forward to decide how this new venture could enhance the community they were building. "I've never seen so many high-powered people," said one, "sitting around a table talking about such a low-budget organization and caring so much about it."

The replication and occasional discontinuation of chapters across the country proceeded over the years, bringing ALF into its fourth decade of service with chapters thriving and fortifying the communities of Houston, Texas; the state of Oregon; Silicon Valley, California; Tacoma/Pierce County, Washington; Charlotte, North Carolina; the Waccamaw region of South Carolina; Sacramento, California (known as Mountain Valley); Modesto, California (known as Great Valley); and East Lansing, Michigan. ALF's four thousand senior fellows come together in countless collaborations for the good of their communities. The theory of change that animates this work is the focus of our next chapter.

CHAPTER 2:
THE ALF THEORY OF CHANGE

"...leadership of trailblazers...is so 'situational' that it rarely draws on known models. Rather it seems to be a fresh creative response to here and now opportunities. Too much concern with how others did it may be inhibitive."

—Robert Greenleaf, *The Servant as Leader*

THERE'S A CONVERSATION that takes place in every community that has an ALF chapter, when a senior fellow recommends the program to a friend or professional associate. It's likely to go something like this:

> "ALF's extraordinary. It's really had a major impact on me. And I think you'd be a good fit for the program. You'd get a lot out of it, and you'd have a lot to contribute to the class."
>
> "That's that thing you go off and do every month, right?"
>
> "Right."
>
> "For a whole year, right?"
>
> "Yes, plus the week we spend together out in nature. And after the first year we collaborate on some work together."
>
> "Wow. I can't really imagine finding that much time. I have trouble covering all the bases as it is right now."

"It is a lot of time, that's true. I didn't know how I'd pull it off at the beginning, but somehow I did. And it was completely worth it."

"Why? What's so special about it?"

Here there's a pause. The senior fellow might have a highlight or outcome from the ALF year to share, but the gist of the answer has often been, "I can't exactly explain it. You have to believe me. It works, it just does. You'll understand the power of ALF after you've done it."

> "ALF doesn't make sense until the end. It proves out the saying 'trust the process.' If you don't, you're going to wonder what it is and why you're doing all this. At the end, you know."
>
> —Jonathan Kresken, ALF-Waccamaw

Plenty of senior fellows have found this testimonial to be true. They enter the program, fueled by their trust in a friend's judgment, with scant understanding of what the year will bring. They finish it struck by the impact the experience has had on their lives and work, and might find they are ready to tell another friend or colleague, "Trust me. It works."

While ALF's "secret sauce," as some have lightly called it, has been adequate to sustain the recruitment of new participants from one year to the next, it falls short of contributing to the larger conversation of the why and how of collaborative leadership development. More importantly, it hampers replication of the work in other communities. What replication requires is a theory of change that can be articulated and conveyed effectively without leaning solely on the personal capital of *trust me*.

A look at ALF's theory of change helps to make clear the path it takes to reach its ultimate outcome: healthy and vibrant communities.

ASSUMPTIONS

Jaworski founded ALF based on several assumptions. He had a fundamental belief that communities would only get better if leaders who had developed a significant sphere of influence came together. He held firm to his assumption that time was needed to develop deep connections, and that like-minded people could never accomplish as much as groups that integrated diverse points of view. Jaworski also described the focus of the necessary work in terms of a set of cornerstones that have evolved over time into five key values: primacy of relationship; appreciation, exploration, and inclusion of diversity; dialogue and collaboration; service to the common good; and inner reflection and personal growth.

Working from these assumptions, ALF's Theory of Change is captured here:

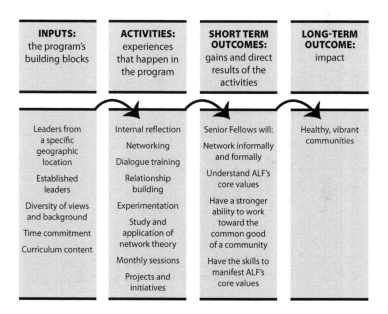

INPUTS: the program's building blocks	ACTIVITIES: experiences that happen in the program	SHORT TERM OUTCOMES: gains and direct results of the activities	LONG-TERM OUTCOME: impact
Leaders from a specific geographic location	Internal reflection	Senior Fellows will:	Healthy, vibrant communities
	Networking	Network informally and formally	
	Dialogue training		
Established leaders	Relationship building	Understand ALF's core values	
Diversity of views and background	Experimentation	Have a stronger ability to work toward the common good of a community	
Time commitment	Study and application of network theory		
Curriculum content	Monthly sessions	Have the skills to manifest ALF's core values	
	Projects and initiatives		

INPUTS

For the most part, ALF's necessary inputs were clear to Jaworski and his colleagues before the first class ever convened. They were design features that naturally emerged from their belief in servant leadership, and in the conditions necessary to nurture it: carefully-developed personal relationships, past leadership experience, awareness of the importance of diversity and the vital nourishment of inner reflection.

THE IMPORTANCE OF GEOGRAPHIC COMMUNITY

From the beginning, ALF grounded its work in a discrete and definable place. This required no rigorous analysis; geographic communities are plainly where strong interpersonal connections are most easily created.

SELECTING FOR LEADERSHIP EXPERIENCE

As important as identification with literal place, of course, is the matter of who came together. ALF's founders believed that if a cross-section of a community's business, elected, academic, non-profit, professional, arts, union, government/political, and religious leaders could be brought together to work on public issues, the potential quality of collaborative achievement would be nearly unlimited.

"The small group is the unit of transformation. It is the structure that allows every voice to be heard."

—Peter Block, *Community*

Every ALF class has about twenty members who are selected with careful intention, usually by senior fellows in the chapter. Those chosen are already established leaders, people who have records of achievement in their particular sectors of influence and a vested interest in the well-being of their communities.

The practice of enlisting influential people already "in charge" of something is central to ALF's theory of change. Leaders tend to have networks of their own, which extend ALF's impact well beyond its fellows into the corners of their communities. This is the context in which ALF has been called a *network of networks*.

Although the insistence on previous leadership experience has opened ALF to occasional charges of elitism in the selection process, it offers decisive advantages:

- Each class is a group of relative equals who are comfortable with power and influence. No one can readily coerce or impress through perceived power—or hide from it—because everyone carries into the program the experience of power. Some of the activities they experience through the year (detailed in Chapter 3) are designed to further level the playing field, paring back the divisive power of title, position, or perceived influence in the community.

- Everyone arrives with considerable leadership background, in both theory and practice. ALF fellows have participated in any number of leadership trainings, seminars, and retreats. Many can readily tell you their Myers-Briggs type, their DiSC profile, and conflict style. They've had the experience of 360-degree feedback, whether or not they asked for it. They have a good idea of what they're getting into; if they agree to enter the ALF program, they are ready to go deeper and faster.

- Everyone has experienced joys, hardships, and successes in life, all of which help impart an understanding of the complexity of community change.

INCLUSION OF DIVERSE VIEWS AND BACKGROUNDS

It is not difficult to convene a group of established leaders who think and see the world similarly; they can be found preassembled in corporate suites and nonprofit boardrooms. But members of communities where ALF chapters are found, like communities everywhere, see the world differently. An ALF class can offer significant value to its community only if it reflects that diversity.

"The world has changed," says Mel Taylor (ALF-Houston). "It is not just changing, it *has changed*. We are a nation of many, many different people of many, many different beliefs. Those of us who resist those changes are going to be left behind. ALF offers a unique model for embracing the differences and showing the connection that lies underneath the differences. And that sounds like a cliché, but my ALF experience allowed me to feel the underlying connection in a way I otherwise could not have."

A class will include leaders from the government, corporate, small business, and nonprofit sectors, some with official titles and others with more informal influence in their segment of the community. The num-

> *"Everyone you will ever meet knows something you don't."*
> —**William Nye (aka Bill Nye the Science Guy)**

ber of men and women will be close to the same. Fellows tend to range from their late thirties to mid-sixties; as a practical matter, the focus on established leaders with considerable life experience can limit the inclusion of younger people. The racial, ethnic, sexual orientation, religious, political, and economic composition will vary by ALF chapter, reflecting their local communities.

At a new ALF class's first meeting, everyone should be able to see people who appear to be the "other." A high-level energy company executive sits across the table from an environmental activist; a conservative minister meets the leader of the gay and lesbian support center for the first time. Tension at the beginning of the ALF experience is a vital ingredient. As one chapter director likes to say on that first day, "If you can't see at least one person in this class whom you believe you disagree with, we haven't done our recruiting job right."

The practical importance of participant diversity is explored more fully in Chapter 5.

EXPLICIT TIME COMMITMENTS

What would it take to infuse even the most carefully selected leaders with the trust and mutual regard that underpin the visions that Greenleaf, Bohm, and others had sketched? It would take time, and lots of it—exactly the resource in shortest supply for many of the leaders whom ALF wanted to engage.

Convinced that there were no shortcuts to forging personal relationships deep enough to manifest their vision, the founders made a bold decision. Participants would have to find a way to commit to coming together as a group for one to two days a month for a full year, as well as an additional week for an intensive wilderness experience. And most would be expected to participate for a second year, taking on a less strictly-defined obligation to collaboratively design and implement a project of service.

Would all of that be a realistic requirement? Not, as it turned out, for as many community leaders as Jaworski had hoped.

That was the empirical discovery of Joe Synan, ALF's national director in its early years. Synan met with civic leaders across the country to tell ALF's story. "Whenever I told them about Suite 8F," Synan says, "someone around the table would say, 'Oh yeah, we have one of those here. But you know, they don't seem to get that much done anymore.'" Synan's advocacy for a new kind of leadership was well-received, but many he talked to were daunted by the resources and participation commitments that ALF required. Some of those initial conversations led to the founding of year-long civic leadership programs with more modest time requirements. "Some of these turned out to be very good," Synan says. "For some communities, they were simply a more realistic fit."

The weight of this time commitment has been one of the most persistent single challenges facing the ALF program. To have significant impact, the program had to recruit leaders who understood leadership challenges and who had networks that could leverage ALF's investment in them. Almost by definition, these are the people, in Earl Blumenauer's words, "who had real jobs, too many commitments, and no time."

> "There is no shortcut to life. To the end of our days, life is a lesson imperfectly learned."
>
> —Harrison Salisbury, journalist

More than a few accomplished people over the years declined or deferred invitations into the program for this reason alone. Others have accepted, fitting the commitment into their schedules with world-class juggling skills and in some cases selfless support and patience from family members.

ACTIVITIES

ALF brings together diverse, seasoned people from a shared place, and asks them to spend a year together exploring ALF's five core values though activities designed to obtain the ultimate goal of healthy and vibrant communities. The ALF year includes readings, exercises, interactive presentations, and disruptive experiences, such as a week in the wilderness. Highly intentional individual and group practices help the classes develop and maintain deep and strong relationships. And skills development in Dialogue, assessment of leadership styles, and collaborative leadership provide leaders with the tools they need to manifest ALF's five core values in their work.

One of the most intentional activities during the ALF year is the class project. ALF classes have designed and implemented a strikingly broad variety of initiatives and programs targeted at some identified need or challenge in their communities.

In the context of the theory of change, the class project starts out with greater prospects for success because the activities that preceded them nurtured exceptional levels of trust, respect, understanding and—last but definitely not least—patience among the collaborators. These elements of the model will also be described in fuller detail in the next chapter.

SHORT-TERM OUTCOMES AND THE LONG-TERM OUTCOME

The activities predictably move ALF fellows to *short-term outcomes* that begin to manifest the kind of leadership that Jaworski and his colleagues envisioned. Evaluations of the success of ALF programs have been conducted in various chapters, primarily using pre/post survey data and interviews. The findings consistently indicate positive impact. Although the academic rigor of the evaluation varies between ALF chapters, the anecdotal data is consistently overwhelming among all chapters over the past 30 years of the program. Quite simply, a majority of senior fellows stays connected to their ALF networks both informally and formally and report a stronger

ability to work toward the common good of the community.

These outcomes, as they pro-
liferate, deepen and mature, are
the catalytic ingredients for our
long-term outcome, the defining
reason for ALF's existence—and
perhaps your interest in this
book—healthy and vibrant communities. While this outcome
is subjective and challenging to measure, civic leaders around
the country would have no trouble pointing out ways in which
senior fellow collaborations have moved their communities towards that ideal.

> *"Leadership isn't about
> any formula. It's about life
> throwing things in your
> way, and how you're
> going to deal with them."*
> —**Vickie Chamberlain,**
> **ALF-Oregon**

NOT QUITE ENOUGH

A theory of change helps us understand the path leading to the
ultimate goal of ALF—healthy, vibrant communities—but does
not explain the profound shifts that individuals, and the group as
a whole, experience during the year. The explanation for why so
many senior fellows come out of ALF deeply impacted both personally and in their stance as community leaders has remained
elusive, frustrating everyone who *knows* the program works.

This sense that a piece was missing followed ALF through its
first two decades. Then along came a conceptual model, in part
from the work of ALF's primary founder, which brought greater
precision to the organization's understanding of why ALF worked.

THE U PROCESS CURVE

Jaworski never lost his drive to learn, and over the years he
continued to explore many of the same themes he described in
Synchronicity. Essential among these were the power of reflection
to connect us to a presence larger than ourselves and the power
of dialogue to break down barriers between us. His quest brought
him together with others seeking to understand the nature of
organizational change, including Peter Senge and international

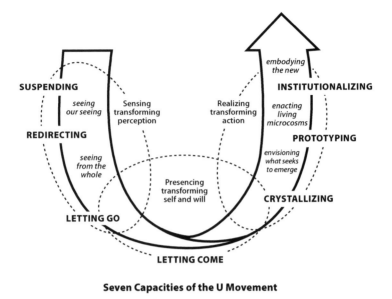

Seven Capacities of the U Movement

From *Presence: An Exploration of Profound Change in People, Organizations, and Society* by Peter Senge, C. Otto Scharmer, Joseph Jaworski, Betty Sue Flowers

researcher C. Otto Scharmer, noted for his innovative thinking on leadership models. In 2004 these three, along with author Betty Sue Flowers, published the book *Presence*, which conceptualizes what has been alternately called U theory, U movement, U process and even, in later work by Jaworski, generative discovery. We will refer to this theory as the U process.

The name for this theory came almost inevitably from the graphic representation used to convey the feel of the psychological journey they were describing.

With the emergence of the U process, trainers and leaders within the ALF community had a tool for more fully explaining the work of ALF. Suddenly the secret sauce was much less secret. They had a deeper conscious understanding of *why* what worked so well actually worked.

The authors of *Presence* believe a key challenge for all leaders is to know themselves deeply and to also understand their part of the whole. Scharmer states that we all have "blind spots"—an inability to understand how we see the world through our own particular lenses and to understand how we impact others. When leaders come together to impact their businesses or communities without having full awareness of their blind spots, the ability to move ahead can be limited. The U process is designed to reveal the lenses through which we view the world.

The U process is complex, and one can find any number of detailed descriptions. Simply stated in Jaworski's words, the U process results in "a profound opening of the heart, carried into action." Scharmer offers a guide's commentary on the journey in an online summary of the U process:

> "Everyone needs to struggle with the question of what kind of future we want to create, and that vision is something that is alive and open to change."
>
> **—Peter Block,**
> **Flawless Consulting**

> We move down one side of the U (connecting us to the world that is outside of our institutional bubble) to the bottom of the U (connecting us to the world that emerges from within) and up the other side of the U (bringing forth the new into the world). On that journey, at the bottom of the U, lies an inner gate that requires us to drop everything that isn't essential. This process of letting-go (of our old ego and self) and letting-come (our highest future possibility: our Self) establishes a subtle connection to a deeper source of knowing. The essence of presencing is that these two selves—our current self and our best future Self—meet at the bottom of the U and begin to listen and resonate with each other. Once a group crosses this threshold, nothing remains the same. Individual members and the group as a whole begin to operate with a heightened level of energy and sense of future possibility. Often they then begin to function as an intentional vehicle for an emerging future.

John Hollar (ALF-Silicon Valley) thinks of the movement down the left side of the U as a process of "building a personal capacity for awareness," as well as:

> a willingness to understand and consciously overcome limitations that often masquerade as experience, intuition or even just memory. [Otto] Scharmer calls this the "open mind, open heart, open will" approach. He describes it as the antidote to believing we see or know more than we really do, or that we can predict the future based on what we know rather than simply paying attention, and being open.

> *"When one can no longer see, one can at least know."*
> —**Joseph Jaworski,** *Synchronicity*

Though the previous diagram seems fairly straightforward, the process is not in fact linear—parts of this process can and usually do occur simultaneously. New self-awareness and group dynamics emerge (or retreat into occasional chaos) such that the group might circle in place or double back (noted by the circles in the diagram) to an earlier position, even as the larger movement through the U inexorably continues. Individuals enter the ALF program with a strong sense of self, distinct from others in the class, with their "blind spots" intact. Through the year, individuals move into deeper relationships with other class members, while simultaneously learning about themselves. At the bottom of the U, the trust and connection opens the group up to the possibility of co-creating change.

How does that happen? Let's follow the U through the major programmatic elements of an ALF year.

CHAPTER 3:
THE ALF YEAR

A COLLECTION OF TWENTY-SOME community leaders file into a room together for the first time. They have all accepted invitations to enter a new class of the American Leadership Forum. Some will see a friend or two in the room, and perhaps a few more familiar faces. For the most part, the people they are meeting are only known to them through what they have read or heard from others in the community.

They know that these people will become more important in their lives. They're going to be spending a lot of time together in ways designed to place them in deep relationships. They know that an ultimate goal is to serve their community more effectively. And busy, accomplished people that they are, they naturally hope to pursue that goal *efficiently*.

What they don't know is that they are perched on the top of the left side of the U. As much as they'd like their new cohort of colleagues to move straight across to the outcome of a healthier, more vibrant community—the shortest distance between two points is, after all, a straight line— that's not what's about to happen. The experiences of ALF's founders, of the originators of U process, and of countless senior fellows, all lead to

> *"I remember on the first day as we met people, thinking, 'I wonder what I'll think of this person a year from now?'"*
>
> **—Judy Wallis ALF-Houston**

a shared conclusion: the straight line simply does not lead to the sustained civic engagement and quality of community we all seek.

> "I like to think of the U Process during the ALF Program in three parts, with each part framed by a single question. Who am I? forms the initial exploration; Who am I with you? is the second question; and finally comes What is possible for you and I to achieve together?"
>
> —**Robin Teater, Executive Director, ALF-Oregon**

The first meeting of an ALF class is highly memorable for most senior fellows. Some have already begun "the letting-go" inherent to the left side of the U; others hold an unsettling suspicion that a grave mistake has been made.

Claire Spain-Rémy (ALF-Tacoma) says that the first thing she noticed was the list of her prospective classmates, a cross-section of her community's most successful business, non-profit and government leaders:

> Now, *that* was intimidating. These people had all led something big or donated large amounts of time and talent to their communities. How did I get in here? What did I have to offer? I was just a local doctor whose fledgling attempts at leadership had been positions on medical staff committees and running a small practice.
>
> Obviously for them this was going to be a refresher course, or maybe a sharing of techniques and best practices. What would I have in common with them? Who thought it was a good idea to put all of these people together in the same rooms many days over the course of a year? And how could we all spend a week together in the wilderness?"
>
> **Claire Spain-Rémy, MD, is senior vice president for MultiCare Medical Associates and lives in Lakewood, Washington.**

At this first gathering the class might be given a short history of ALF and the rationale for the program, a schedule that lists a topical focus for the year's monthly meetings, and a basic syllabus listing speakers, trainers and readings. These will inform their experience along the way, but they won't propel it. With the help of intentionally-designed activities and environments, the participants themselves will propel it. "Sometimes you'll hear critical comments from some of the more analytical folks," says a facilitator who's worked with dozens of ALF classes over the years. "They might say that the curriculum or data doesn't seem to hang together in a highly coherent way. Then at some point in the year there'll be a shift, and they suddenly realize, 'Oh! *We're* the curriculum. *We're* the data.'"

The U-shaped journey on which they're embarking is by definition emergent and unpredictable—exactly like the actual practice of leadership in their lives as citizens and professionals. The arc will vary from chapter to chapter and class to class, and, to some degree, from one individual class-member to the next. The location of this learning community on the U at any given time depends on the state of individual and group consciousness. The fluid nature of the U process calls for adept process management and emotional intelligence, in addition to a content expertise in leadership development.

What follows is a description of common ALF practices that have been found to be useful in guiding classes down, across and back up the U. They have been developed in various ALF chapters over the last three decades and continue to evolve.

STARTING DOWN THE U: SUSPENDING AND REDIRECTING

The initial journey down the left side of the U centers on individuals discovering common ground, learning about their impact on others, and experiencing how a community operates as a complex system. The ALF class is a microcosm of the community they all live in and creates the perfect container for the initial movement down the U.

Suspending and redirecting is all about, first and foremost, becoming open to the idea that there are different ways to see the world than the view I hold, and I most likely do not have any awareness of this fact. The suspension of our own belief that we are "right" leads to opportunities to learn about oneself and others through reflection, observation of others, stringent attention to listening, and the practice of an intentional model of Dialogue. The role of a facilitator in this part of the U process is described by Scharmer:

> First, you help the group *suspend* judgments in order to see the objective reality they are up against, including the basic figures and facts. Second, you help them *redirect* their attention from the object to the process in order to help them view the system from a perspective that allows them to see how their own actions contribute to the problem at hand. It is at that point that people begin to see themselves as part of the issue, they begin to see how they collectively create a pattern that at first seemed to be caused by purely exterior forces. And then, if you are lucky, you can bring them to a *deeper place of stillness* where they let go of the old and start to connect with their higher order intentions.
>
> **—Otto Scharmer,** *Theory U*

Suspending and redirecting are encouraged with several specific approaches within the ALF program.

THE BUDDY SYSTEM

The suggestion that a group of people you are about to meet will become important in your life and your work can unnerve the most confident and socially graceful incoming ALF fellow. It's a moment where most people would feel strengthened by the support of a colleague and friend. With this in mind, every class member is paired with a "buddy," determined either by random lot or by intentional assignment. Class buddies can make the journey safer and help each other process the experience as it unfolds.

"I couldn't believe at first who they chose to be my buddy," says a Houston fellow. "I had dealings with him before, and we were from different *planets.* I just couldn't imagine what they were thinking. But about midway through the program, what they were thinking became very clear."

THE SEVEN MINUTE TALK

The centerpiece of that first class meeting is usually an exercise known plainly enough as the seven minute talk. Each participant is asked to answer a short list of questions in no more than seven minutes. Some respond simply in words, others bring in pictures, and some write a piece of poetry or music.

> *"With the boundaries set for some safety, you can really get a long ways toward building relationship in seven minutes."*
>
> **—Jonathan Kresken, ALF-Waccamaw**

The questions vary over time, but these from ALF's Silicon Valley chapter are typical:

- Which people and what experiences have influenced you most powerfully?

- What moments stand out as critical to who you are and what you care about?

- How do you want to serve in our community and the world; what will your legacy be?

The format seems to trigger a kind of mutual recognition that dissolves ordinary barriers. "Hearing right from the start about our personal lives—our kids, what was really important to us, all of that—was important," says Denise Bradley (ALF-Houston). "That immediately got me through stereotypes I'd brought with me without knowing it, especially about my buddy, an imposing African American man I didn't think I had anything in common with."

Claire Spain-Rémy (ALF-Tacoma) vividly remembers writing out what she planned to say in her talk. As she waited for her turn she wondered what this roomful of important strangers would think of what she planned to tell them:

> Then someone opened up and gave a piece of their soul. A dam burst and more deep emotions, wounds, and hopes poured forth. I can still remember where each person sat and the stories they told. Stories that moved me and sometimes the

speaker to tears. Stories about the relationships that they longed for with family members who were no longer there. Stories about having to deal with the murder of a parent, the loss of a marriage, the lack of acceptance of their life choices by people that

> ...It doesn't interest me
> where or what or with whom
> you have studied.
> I want to know
> what sustains you
> from the inside
> when all else falls away....
>
> —From the poem *The Invitation*,
>   Oriah Mountain Dreamer

mattered to them. A story about marrying the love of your life even though you know they are dying. Stories about growing up with nothing or living with abuse or physical or emotional neglect. And I told mine, the story of a young black girl growing up in one of the most segregated cities in the United States during the civil rights movement. They listened to my shaky and emotion-laden voice and cared about what I had to say.

Why were people who knew very little about each other willing to do this? Maybe because they, like me, felt a need to be heard. Maybe they, like me, had become successful and felt that it was necessary to bury and hide these feelings, because to speak of them or dwell on them could be seen as a sign of weakness in a leader. In that session we started to bond and laid a foundation for openness, honesty, and self-examination. It didn't all happen at once but there was a linkage starting to form.

Beyond its potency for initiating strong relationships, the seven minute talk begins breaking ground for the more private internal work that awaits further down the U. The envelope of disclosure, familiarity, and acceptance that begins to take form with this opening exercise is the foundation for an environment that will invite deeper reflection on one's own life and leadership journey than some fellows have experienced before.

CHECK-INS

The intention of the seven minute talk is carried through the year by the consistent practice of checking in. Whenever the class reconvenes after time apart, the first group process is usually a round in which everyone speaks without interruption on what is currently compelling in their life.

The focus is sometimes physical, emotional, or mental challenges, sometimes workplace or personal setbacks or triumphs and sometimes stories of celebration or appreciation. Often, check-ins are reports of inner shifts or moments of awareness that are intensely personal and rarely revealed in peer-to-peer conversation. Fellows rely on this practice to be a moment to reconnect with their classmates and with their commitment to the process; it is an intentional moment when they leave behind the noise and agitation of their busy lives to become fully present for the group.

"You're forced to hard places sometimes, sides of your situation or personality you don't want to face. Sometimes you're pushed to take a stand you never have before....there's a chance to get feedback about who you are in a group that you don't get anywhere else—not in your own organization, even when you're seeking feedback from people you work with. Because we build such a high level of trust—even love—we can accept and hear that feedback. I had classmates come to me so grateful that I was willing to say what I did to them."

—Cynthia Elsberry, ALF-Waccamaw

Whether because of a shared interest in making the most of that time, or the depths plumbed by courageous members of the group, the check-ins often reach a depth of intimacy and self-revelation that is striking. "I don't know how the trust level builds up so high so fast," said a Charlotte class member. "But it does."

When a workplace challenge surfaces during the check-in, it may be set aside for further attention later. It's not unusual for a class member's professional puzzle to become a case study for the class—both a learning opportunity for the group and a direct near-term benefit for the person who brought it in.

A DISRUPTIVE EXPERIENCE

Talk to any senior fellow about ALF and you are almost certain to hear about the intensive time his or her class spent over the course of a week together. Jaworski originally conceived of this segment of the program as an Outward Bound-style week in a wilderness [or "natural outdoor"] setting. In *Synchronicity* he lists five objectives that informed its design:

- Strengthen the fellows' power of self-belief, their feeling of self-efficacy, and the belief that they can accomplish what they set forth to do. It was our intent to give them the clear message that they were using only a fraction of their true capacity. We then would give them solid evidence of that fact.

- Encourage the fellows to rely on their inner resources that are so seldom tapped, to use their intuition and the ability to extemporize and innovate in the face of uncertainty and ambiguity.

- Build deep trust and respect among the group, and help each fellow get beyond the devaluing prejudices that we all hold. Build true teamwork among the group and have them experience—perhaps for the first time—what deep alignment in a group feels like. Foster an experience of how a group of leaders from many sectors in a community can coalesce around issues of shared concern and move to successful resolution.

- Put the fellows in situations that will cause them to reach deeply into themselves and be led into what Bohm called "the generating depth of consciousness which is common to the whole of mankind." Evoke their higher nature and have them experience that we are all connected.

- Learn from the entire experience how to be flexible and adapt quickly to change and new environments.

In recent years, different chapters have adapted the original wilderness experience in any number of ways. What characterizes all of them is the idea of a "disruptive experience"—a taking away of what is familiar and comfortable and immersing class members into an intensive week of physical, mental and emotional challenges. All chapters continue to hold this week in a nature setting—agreeing with the conclusion Jaworski reached so many years ago—that nature provides disruption to our everyday routines *and* a place for contemplation and solace.

Two ALF class facilitators, Greg Ranstrom of Outside Insights and Bill Proudman of Inclusivity LLC have guided dozens of ALF classes through their weeks in the wilderness. Both chronicled what they've observed over the years:

> *"Looking around the bus on the way up to the wilderness week, all you saw was people on their Blackberries or smart phones or iPads, doing their work alone by themselves. On the way back down a few days later, all those things were packed away and people were talking a mile a minute about what they were going to do next."*
>
> **—Jonathan Kresken, ALF-Waccamaw**

Greg: Twenty-four diverse leaders board a motor coach on a Sunday morning in July. They compare their new REI apparel and joke about the experiences they will share together over the next week. Many worry about how much longer their cell phones will function. They already feel closer to each other because they know they are in this together.

The cell phones fail as the scenery changes to the conifers, mountain streams, and granite of these mountains. Quiet conversations replace the nervous chatter.

Bill: Leaders must have a "stretching out of their norm" experience (mentally, physically, socially and spiritually), reflect and assimilate what happened, and then apply the learning moving forward. The wilderness week does just that. A group of initial strangers create a leadership learning laboratory.

Greg: Upon arriving at the lake camp, many find that it is better than anticipated. There are yurts with real beds and electric lamps and the water runs both cold and hot. Settling in takes a little while as the pace of professional life gives way to the rhythms of the mountain. The responsibilities that a few hours ago seemed so important begin to find a new order.

Bill: Many come into this experience feeling mildly intimidated, as in, "I hope I measure up to the person who nominated me."

Greg: The next day, a few who said they would not rock climb or rappel surprise themselves and do more than they dreamed possible. Some find, to their surprise, more pleasure in belaying others than in their own personal achievement.

Each night the dialogue around the campfire deepens. Diverse perspectives pose sharp challenges. But not all is serious dialogue; games, song, and story restore a playful nature to the community.

Bill: The learning process is always dynamic. Often the energy to avoid chaos, messiness, or confrontation is strong. Working their way through the dissonance gives each class a unique set of learning opportunities. Most classes come to realize that leadership is not a binary process, rather a process of managing complexity and ambiguity with multiple paths and approaches.

Greg: Then the class takes on a remarkable three-day experience that includes backpacking to a new location, setting up camp, climbing a peak, and soloing.

After a long hike, the arrival at base camp is celebrated. The new camp offers a daunting view of the peak. Small acts of kindness can be seen as people help each other find comfort in the wilderness.

Then, the group plans the peak ascent for the next morning.

Bill: Finding common purpose and meaning is a challenge. It takes time to come to agreement on what success might look like. Building true community is more than a transactional task; it involves integrating the music of many different songs and rhythms into one melody.

The wilderness week often reconnects people to what they already knew, without awareness of their knowing. Class members almost always walk away with a sense of the power and transformative nature of learning from the experience of the collective. The journey provides clarity for some and frustration for others and sometimes both at the same time. It is important learning that had to be experienced, not just studied.

Greg: Back at base camp final preparations are made for the solo experience. And then, the silence begins. Fellows disperse to a solitary location to stay, anywhere from half a day to a fifteen-hour overnight. Some confront fears of being alone in the woods or alone with their thoughts. Most begin to feel a deep, sacred connection to loved ones, humanity, nature, and higher powers. On reconvening, they speak from the heart of their experience, offering gratitude for the group and the week spent together.

The group has changed. Some tough conversations begun in the wilderness must continue and the group digs into these with a little more grace and capacity to learn than was possible just a month before.

Bill: No matter how it happens, one key result is the fellows' realization that they must personally be the change they wish to see in their world. This change is not to become superman or superwoman, but to lead with greater vulnerability, compassion, and heart.

Not that it's necessary to hang from a rope to feel the shift. "I pride myself on not relying on others," says Cynthia Elsberry (ALF-Waccamaw). "And I'm a pretty fit person, so I let myself take a few extra things in my pack for the hike. When we got there,

> *"Doing something in a group that I would and could never do alone was magical."*
>
> **—Bruce W. Davis, ALF-Silicon Valley**

it was too heavy for me to get on my shoulders, and someone stepped right up and helped get it on my back. And right then, immediately, I got it."

Beth Quill (ALF-Houston) describes what the experience reaffirmed for her with an economy of words: "Accept help. No one does it all."

EXPLORING LEADING ACROSS DIFFERENCES

Appreciation, exploration and inclusion of diversity play a key role in helping fellows moving through suspending and re-directing. Chapters facilitate the movement of fellows down the U with activities expressly designed to jar their perspectives and beliefs, and to crack the barriers to understanding completely unfamiliar views of the world.

> "I love people who think things I don't, who can see what's in my blind spot. Together you can pretty much eliminate the blind spots, keep each other out of trouble— you can be early warning systems for each other, and make much better decisions."
>
> —Sarah Smith, ALF-Waccamaw

In some cases this is a formal program element called "experience-as-other" where fellows engage in an experience far removed from their own realities.

"For me, this was vital," says John Breckenridge (ALF-Houston):

> I spent every morning for a week at a school that taught performing arts classes to children with disabilities. Some disabilities were minor and others were severe. Working in the entertainment industry myself, I had a pretty clear-cut preconception of what these kids would and wouldn't be able to do.
>
> And I couldn't have been more wrong. Children who wouldn't talk would all of a sudden break into song. Kids who were bouncing off the walls with ADD behavior calmed when music was introduced. Kids who couldn't carry on a conversation were capable of lines of dialogue in a script. The bond built in that week with the kids and staff led to merger talks between our two organizations. My nonprofit absorbed the small teaching nonprofit into our operations and increased their ability to deliver exponentially.

This is one of several exercises that challenges each ALF cohort to explore deeply the realities of white privilege, institutional bias, and a range of other conditions in the social environment that hamper the ability to work effectively with a thoroughly diverse community of leaders. Some chapters spend a whole day exploring power dynamics across differences; others build the topic into an in-depth look at systems thinking; and others use the immersion week to highlight the way our differences play out in a community.

DIALOGUE

It would be hard to overstate the importance of the Dialogue model to ALF's theory of change and practices. In contrast to how the word is popularly used, generally with a lower case "d," Dialogue is a particular practice that focuses far more on how we listen and respond than how we talk. Dialogue, as we will see in Chapter 6, is actually one of the organization's core values.

Perhaps more than any other, this is the practice that reflects the rhythm and nominal "inefficiency" of the U process. Effective Dialogue demands a sustained commitment of time and energy. "A Dialogue that occurs in a vacuum as a 'one off' conversation, no matter how meaningful," says ALF-Silicon Valley director Chris Block, "does not lead to the deep and trusting relationships necessary to solve the most complex problems that face contemporary society." He acknowledges that the practice isn't universally praised:

> People are often frustrated by this approach and tell ALF, "You place too much emphasis on conversation. You place too much emphasis on Dialogue." Of course at ALF we don't believe—in a world where people get beat up or in a world where people are dying of hunger or in a world where we can't pass a state budget—that we should all get together in a room, in a vacuum, and have a conversation about this or that. That would be to fiddle while Rome burns.
>
> We do believe that it begins with a conversation because that's how people begin significant relationships. The way that people initially come into relationship with one another is through a conversation that allows people to understand each other. This is especially important in extremely diverse

communities where people do not necessarily look like each other and often share a very different life experience. It is Dialogue, not debate, which allows us to build the authentic relationships that are essential if diverse cultures are to solve complex problems.

Kevin McCarthy, a practiced facilitator of ALF, often notes that "...in a debate, we argue our point of view in an effort to prove the rightness of our position and argue against the perspective of others who disagree. We disagree in an effort to strengthen our argument and to persuade others to agree with our original point of view. In Dialogue, diverse perspectives are held together in an effort to explore the complexity of an issue and to discover opportunities for change. In debate we ask *Who is winning?* In Dialogue we ask *What am I learning and where can change occur?*"

MOVING INTO THE BOTTOM: LETTING GO AND PRESENCING

The U process has no crisp corners. Its sides flow seamlessly into the bottom rather than beginning and ending there. The left side's focus on fully *sensing* others while connecting with oneself is not wholly separable from the bottom's *presencing*, the fuller exploration of the self and its source of inspiration.

This transitional bend to the right is the "letting-go" zone, and it can occur spontaneously, unfolding outside any programmatic timeline. At the same time, there are consciously designed elements of the ALF year that support the class members' connection to their sources of inspiration as they move across the bottom of the U.

One feature of the ALF experience that sometimes contributes to the U process is that it can be *fun*. Along with severe demands on her intelligence and sense of identity, Claire Spain-Rémy remembers "the poker parties, good food, good wine, and good music. Where else could I have had the man with the most perfect hair I had ever seen be one of the backup singers to my version of *Ain't No Mountain High Enough?*"

"ALF saved my life," says Dorothy Gibbons (ALF-Houston). "After 25 years of being the CEO, I was worn down, beaten, and didn't feel there would ever be anything that could restore my passion and enthusiasm. ALF gave me a safe space to go vent, to play, to discuss my issues and concerns with like-minded and incredibly smart people."

LEADERSHIP STYLE ASSESSMENT TOOLS

One program element that bolsters both the observation focus of the left side and the inner exploration element of the bottom of the U comes straight from the world of organizational development. Many ALF chapters devote a session to a formal assessment of its members' working styles. The three instruments most frequently used are:

- Myers-Briggs
- DiSC Behavioral profile
- StrengthsFinder

It's not uncommon to hear an initial grumble or two from some who've taken these assessments before, or who don't want to be "pigeonholed." But when understood in the context of effectively harnessing the assets of a diverse team, that resistance often dissolves. This can be especially true after the wilderness experience, when the diversity of individual strengths comes into focus, along with the potential for meshing them strategically to advance the group's goal.

Rather than setting limitations, personality profiles can be aggregated as a kind of inventory of resources available to the group, a guide for matching people to tasks in the most effective way.

DROPPING DOWN DEEPER

The journey to "connect within" soon goes deeper than the categorizations offered by the organizational assessment tools. One objective of ALF's program is to support leaders in better understanding their personal psychological and emotional makeup, including the ways in which they experience and respond to conflict, stress, desires to control, opportunity and issues of personal integrity.

A framework valued by some ALF chapters is introductory aikido. Aikido is performed by blending with the motion of the attacker and redirecting the force of the attack rather than opposing it head-on. Many ALF groups use the practice of aikido as a metaphor for embodying leadership presence. It is used to explore resistance, connection, power and presence in transforming the energy of conflict into purposeful action. Fellows practice these concepts in physical ways and are invited to incorporate them into a more powerful leadership stance. The metaphor for those wanting to have positive impact in a contentious world is powerfully evident.

Fellows have an opportunity to reflect on some of their most difficult professional and personal challenges through the lens of aikido. More than a few have reported breakthroughs in situations that had seemed irresolvable.

Wayne Clark (ALF-Oregon), describing a hostile challenge to his organization, writes: "A force was coming at me with anger, and instead of standing in front of it and trying to push it away or block it, I embraced it and went with it, turning its energy into something positive."

> *From Aikido we learn:*
> *"From a position of awareness and acceptance, a leader can mindfully influence a situation, rather than mindlessly react to it. I believe that this is the essence of personal responsibility."*
>
> **—Drew Hansen, "Study Aikido To Become A Better Business Leader,"** *Forbes,* **December 17, 2012**

REFLECTION AND CONTEMPLATIVE PRACTICES

Few secular groups of successful professionals make a regular practice of incorporating contemplative time when they convene. Most ALF chapters do. In the midst of the cognitive stimulation that is invariably part of the monthly gatherings—sharp encounters of differing world views, intense conceptual brainstorming, first-person storytelling—the centering value of silence and stillness is understood and embraced. Short intervals are often provided to draw inward and increase awareness of the moment. And fellows have been known to push others to "go inside" on a regular basis with some kind of contemplative practice, the kind of habit that tends to get short shrift in the pressured workaday lives of many people.

> *"Pacing oneself by appropriate withdrawal is one of the best approaches to making optimal use of one's resources. The servant-as-leader must constantly ask: How can I use myself to serve best?"*
>
> **—Robert Greenleaf,**
> ***The Servant as Leader***

ALF's contemplative practices strive towards achievement of mindfulness, sometimes described as the art of being fully present. This is what empowers fellows to improve both their personal health and leadership presence. Mindfulness teaches fellows to take a moment to become present and prepare themselves to truly engage in the relationships and dialogues taking place in their ALF sessions, as well as in their personal and professional lives. It creates a physical, emotional and mental shift that prepares each person to see things differently and be more open to possibility. Practices such as mindful stopping, conscious breathing, non-judging awareness, stretching, mindful listening, mindful eating and walking mediation are common in some ALF chapters.

One specific element of ALF's disruptive experience week has been an extraordinary catalyst for internal exploration. It is *the solo*, when fellows disperse to separate locations for anywhere from half a day to a fifteen-hour overnight, with none of the distracting stimulations we usually have around us. "It's often the richest part," says facilita-

> *"Mindfulness means paying attention in a particular way: on purpose, in the present moment, and non-judgementally."*
>
> **—Jon Kabat-Zinn,**
> ***Wherever You Go, There You Are***

tor Bill Proudman, "for hard-driving Type-As who go into it kicking and screaming, or not at all. It's a moment off the treadmill, which a lot of us have gradually cranked up to setting 5, 6 or 7 without even realizing it."

The solo comes up regularly when fellows review their ALF experience. Mary Lynne Calhoun (ALF-Charlotte) writes that it "let me know how hungry I am for solitude and time to reflect, largely absent from my complicated life. I have intentionally sought opportunities for quiet reflection, including a three-day personal retreat in a monastic setting, since gaining that insight."

And Ken Lambla (ALF-Charlotte) immediately saw the piece that his night alone in the wilderness plays in the ALF picture. Getting inside oneself, he says, "is a prerequisite to getting inside others. Getting inside others is to appreciate how much respect is necessary for good, hard, difficult work in the community to be done."

While the self-exploration experience at the bottom of the U never completely ends for those in service to the common good, the wilderness solo experience and mindfulness practice seem to ignite a sense of connection and possibility that helps to power the ascent up the right side.

MOVING UP THE RIGHT SIDE:
CRYSTALLIZING, PROTOTYPING, INSTITUTIONALIZING

If there is a signature moment in the ALF year that most commonly initiates the upward sweep from the U's bottom into the right side's domain of coming together to co-create with others, it might be the connections that fellows form after returning from a week together. Because the disruptive experience week comes early in the ALF timeframe, the class often bonds quickly. The added layers of Dialogue, self-assessment, check-in, and topics such as leading across differences, move the class into action.

This transition at the bottom right of the curve is crucial to the ALF class' experience. After all they have observed with fresh eyes and heard with fresh ears on the left side, after all they've unearthed at the bottom about themselves and their relationship to their animating source, will they come back together with greater capacity to serve the common good? The ALF Leadership in Action initiative lets them find out.

LEADERSHIP IN ACTION

ALF's original format mandates every class to select, design and implement a collaborative change initiative, often called the "class project." The project can be any enterprise that will in some way serve the fellows' larger community.

Typically eight to ten months into the program year, a concentrated effort to select a project begins. This is rarely as easy or straightforward as it might sound. Among twenty or so fellows there will be markedly different areas of interest, levels of patience with process, natural passions, constituencies with urgent needs for support, and levels of demand on their time, from heavy to impossibly heavy.

Navigating these differences moves the class further up into the U's zone of co-creation. At the outset, classes strive to make sure all of their members will be engaged in ways best suited to their strengths and ability to contribute. They also want to be sure their project matters, that their investment of time and energy will have an impact of material value to their communities.

In this navigation, Dialogue is an essential tool, and the outcome can be illuminating. "There are definitely magic moments," says Joe Synan, ALF's former national director. "After an intense, draining session or two, when agreement is finally reached on the project focus, somebody will lean back, take a deep breath, and say, 'Wow. I've never seen a decision made that way before.'" Over the years, Joe has facilitated dozens of ALF class sessions aimed at selecting a project. In his view the projects were not always "roaring successes" in terms of measurable outcomes. "There was always a tension between *process* and *product*," he says. Synan continues:

> After a while the purpose of this segment in the overall program became clearer and clearer. It was not a "performance." It was instead a test case for the capacity of this diverse group to put into practice the fundamental purpose of the ALF

program: joining and strengthening leaders to better serve the public good.

Senior fellows often cited the project as the most difficult and uncomfortable part of the ALF program. Simultaneously they often said it was the aspect of the program that was the best opportunity for the participants to strengthen their capacity to be community leaders.

In evaluating the efficacy of the project to move fellows up the right side of the U, chapters have considered not only the impact of the process on fellows, but the value of the projects themselves. Senior fellows' assessments of the success of their class projects vary. Some claim success. Some would have liked to see more ambitious and consequential projects selected. Sometimes participation was uneven, with a small number of fellows carrying the load while others disengaged. Classes wrestled with, and didn't always reconcile, philosophical differences in how best to approach community change.

ALF chapters have been exploring other means for helping fellows journey through the co-creating portion of the U to achieve the kind of impact for which the process is designed. The growing focus on the power of networks has led to some interesting experimentation in how to better bring the assets of the ALF classes to bear on community issues. Current approaches include engaging fellows in smaller projects, self-organized by interest, and in creating new networks of networks which can be mobilized as needs arise.

GROWING THE IMPACT

Growing the impact of the senior fellow network is an active, intentional, and challenging process and involves two strategies. The first strategy is to bring senior fellows together to renew, sustain and expand the personal relationships that are the network's key ingredient.

Most gatherings of ALF senior fellows embody the U process all over again—where individuals find themselves once again connecting in ways that allow a rapid ride on the U. ALF chapters invite graduates from all of their classes to a variety of gatherings. These might be lectures or receptions featuring thought leaders in areas aligned with ALF's areas of interest, weekend trainings, community dialogues or workshops, landmark events of organizations at the center of senior fellows' work, or celebratory fundraising dinners. In one chapter, classes have been convening senior fellow forums focused on vital civic issues.

> "Despite current ads and slogans, the world doesn't change one person at a time. It changes when networks of relationships form among people who share a common cause and vision of what's possible. ... We don't need to convince large numbers of people to change; instead, we need to connect with kindred spirits. Through these relationships, we will develop the new knowledge, practices, courage and commitment that lead to broad-based change."
>
> **—Margaret Wheatley and Deborah Frieze, "Using Emergence to Take Social Innovation to Scale"**

These formal efforts have met with mixed success. Some senior fellows make a priority of sustaining their ALF connections and the opportunities for collaboration that come with them; others find the press of personal and professional demands too extensive to remain active members of the network. Other fellows have active connections, outside of the formal ALF chapter efforts and continue to have an impact that may not be attributed to the ALF network.

The second strategy is to facilitate diverse networking by connecting community leaders across professions, neighborhoods, ethnicities, economic conditions, etc. beyond the class year. In order to do this, some chapters have recently added "single sector" classes to their programming (focused on health care and criminal justice, for example) to determine if common professional interests will sustain collaboration and contribute to the long-term outcome of ALF.

Built on all the assumptions of the traditional ALF class, with one interesting twist—recruitment is done within a sector, such as education, justice system, or health—a single sector class spends a similar year together. Some fellows are recruited from the senior fellow pool while others have never been through the ALF program.

> *"I now am seeing the complexity of the criminal justice system. Being in this class has made me aware that you can't judge change in one part of the system because of the impact you see in other parts of the system. We are allies in the belief that we can solve things together."*
>
> **—Terry O'Rourke, ALF-Houston**

These single sector classes provide an opportunity to create innovation networks, networks whose members share ALF's five core values and have the skills to transform systems. Imagine a year, with judges, advocates, victims, politicians, and defense attorneys all in the same room, wrestling with how to collectively improve the community's justice system.

The growing emphasis in our connected world on the power of networking and personal relationships was realized by ALF years ago. ALF chapters have never stopped exploring new ways to capitalize on both to help senior fellows impact their communities As one former ALF director once said: "The ALF Program is the boot camp. The real work begins once you graduate."

Part II

LEADERSHIP APPLIED: WHEN POWERFUL THEORY MEETS COMPLEX REALITY

IF THE U PROCESS provides a highway map for the "secret sauce," then the most important rules of the road for fellows are ALF's *five core values*. These values, and the stories of ALF senior fellows striving to ground them in their professional and community lives, are our focus in Part II, *Leadership Applied*. The values are:

- The primacy of relationship
- Appreciation, exploration, and inclusion of diversity
- Dialogue and collaboration
- Service to the common good
- Inner reflection and personal growth

In a world of ethical dilemmas, urgent demands and tempting shortcuts, it comes as no surprise that these values can be markedly easier to describe than to apply to daily life. With almost four thousand ALF senior fellows around the county, there was no need to speculate on this challenge of practical application. We simply talked to them.

When we started this book, we asked more than a hundred senior fellows to describe moments that stood out as they carried their ALF experiences back to their communities. Some of them wrote stories to distill what they learned. A sampling of those stories appear in the five following chapters (more can be found at www.everythingweknowaboutleadership.org), organized by the specific value they reflect.

What you are likely to notice is that these stories refuse to fit neatly under any one value. Because the practice of one often leads naturally to the practice of others, the values have a way of blending when they are applied. If you sense that a story in the chapter on diversity could as readily have been placed in the chapter on personal growth, or that collaboration stories are relationship stories, you are on solid ground.

What follows is a very small fraction of the stories that thousands of senior fellows around the nation could tell.

CHAPTER 4:
PRIMACY OF RELATIONSHIP

THERE IS ONE phrase that consistently comes up when senior fellows are asked about their ALF experience: "It's all about relationship."

It is personal relationship that helps actualize ALF's other core values, the practice of which demands a great deal. ALF senior fellows are called on to reexamine and sometimes let go of assumptions, beliefs, and fears that have rooted deeply within them over the course of a lifetime. This is courageous work in uncharted territory. It calls for deeper levels of transparency, acceptance of un-

"We're all just people. Accomplishing extraordinary things is much more about one-on-one relationship than institutions trying to drive change."

—**Lisa Helfman, ALF-Houston**

certainty, and above all, greater personal vulnerability than many people have ever ventured. This is likely to happen only in a well-developed interpersonal "container" of empathy, affection, and trust. ALF strives to provide that container.

Relationship is the raw material of ALF's most intentional product: an expanding network of leaders with shared experience and values, a human infrastructure that serves the common good by using and integrating an array of talents and resources. This network will be only as strong as the personal relationships that make it up. When two or more people with shared commitment to their community develop a strong personal relationship, they become a building block of a sound leadership network.

FROM ADVERSARIES TO ALLIES

Joe Whitworth and Dan Keppen (both ALF-Oregon) took an existing relationship that might be called "polite adversaries" to a very different level during their year together in ALF:

> **Joe Whitworth:** Agriculture and conservation are the two most natural allies that cannot speak each other's language—and precious few translators exist. Because I grew up bucking hay in the Midwest and later became the head of the conservation group that listed the first Pacific Salmon under the Endangered Species Act, I see both sides. While I know deeply that landowners do not wake up in the morning looking to do environmental harm, I also know that financial realities drive how they manage their operation. So the value I bring to this field is in a kind of translation. Thing is, though, one translator needs another to create and sustain breakthroughs. My ALF experience provided the setting for that relationship to be built.
>
> **Dan Keppen:** Joe and I met in 2003, when I was executive director of the Klamath Water Users Association. The issue that brought us together was the same that keeps us both in business: water.
>
> **Joe:** In particularly dry years, with increased pressure on water supplies, farmers predictably dug in on one side, and the "greens" dug in on the other. There was no real dialogue. There were power politics, shout-downs, and litigation. Dan and I found ourselves on panels speaking about our respective interests in the basin. We struck up a relationship built on respect and always talked about finding a way to navigate through the needlessly explosive minefield of agriculture versus conservation, but we never followed through. Whether we were too busy, too far away, or the move was too progressive for our constituencies—we never made it happen. Bottom line is that he and I always knew that our constituencies could easily agree on 70 percent of most issues, but focused on the 30 percent that separated them. And focusing on the

disagreements created fear and mistrust.

Dan: So five years later Joe and I end up in ALF together. There, our professional relationship blossomed into one of friendship, in large part due to the camaraderie of the ALF process. Joe is an accomplished outdoorsman, and I remember having to eat humble pie several times when forced to sheepishly approach him for advice on how to tie knots for our rock-climbing exercise in the Columbia River Gorge. He always helped, but added some good-natured ribbing to let me know where I stood. I pulled a good one on him later, though, when the class came together in a circle. The facilitator whispered a phrase to one of our classmates which we were instructed to pass around the circle from classmate to classmate. By the time the message made it around—with a little help from yours truly—it had morphed from "Trouble is brewing, my friend," to "Joe Whitworth likes barnyard animals." From then on our classmates referred to him as "Barnyard Joe."

Joe: ALF forced us together each month for more than a year in a setting apart from our professional roles and allowed us to expand our relationship into a durable friendship. He gained a good deal of admiration from me through his open approach in dealing with the death of his father, a marital change, and the discovery and correction of a brain aneurysm. He constantly tried to make sense of it and make good use of the learning. His earnestness more than made up for his eighth-grade sense of humor.

Dan: As our ALF friendship grew, so did our mutual trust and respect. Joe and I both recognized that the best opportunities to improve trout habitat were on private lands. For groups like Oregon Trout to maximize habitat potential, private landowners like ranchers need to participate. Those ranchers are going to be much more inclined to participate if they get something in return—maybe another cash flow stream, or maybe environmental credits.

Joe: Our mutual trust gave us a willingness to take risks in bringing the new ideas to the table and focusing on those issues where we agree. We are together making folks first uncomfortable and then comfortable in new territory, focusing on forward solutions rather than more of the same.

Dan: ALF gave me a strong belief that leaders should always be ready to stand up for other leaders. Our two organizations work cooperatively in a variety of political and public forums. We recently co-wrote a guest opinion for *The Oregonian* that focused on the positive aspects of farmer-conservationist partnerships.

Joe: We have some heavy lifts in front of us. Agriculture is at once the most ecologically destructive and humanly critical enterprise on Earth. In the next forty years, we will need to grow as much food as we have in all human history, without destroying the biosphere's capacity to do it thereafter. We are not on track to do that. We can get there, but not through the old conversations and the old ways. Through the new ones. And for that work, I now have an ally to help me rebalance the scales.

Dan: The "farmers vs. fish" dynamic that very likely could have defined our relationship has instead turned into something closer to "farmers for fish." The listening, collaboration, and networking that is such a part of the ALF experience definitely played a large part in the strong personal and professional relationship I have to this day with "Barnyard Joe" Whitworth.

Dan Keppen is executive director of the Family Farm Alliance and lives in Klamath Falls, Oregon. Joe Whitworth is president of The Freshwater Trust and lives in Portland, Oregon.

"WE BELIEVE YOU CAN DO IT"

Judy Wallis (ALF-Houston) comes from a solid line of lifelong learners. "I had a grandmother who matriculated for a third degree from the University of Texas at seventy-two and a father who worked and wrote professionally up until a few months before his death in his late seventies," she says. So Judy felt well-suited for an adventure like ALF relatively late in her career. She says the most powerful learning moment was one she didn't expect. It came after she'd decided, shortly after significant knee surgery, that she would not be able to hike to the top of the mountain with her class:

Ready for the peak, our group set out. From the very beginning of the journey, I moved through the terrain surrounded by support and encouragement from my classmates. As we approached the peak, [Houston ALF chapter director] Harriet Wasserstrum and our guide, who had stayed with me the entire journey, turned to me and spoke six unforgettable words: "We believe you can do it."

It took a moment to realize what she was saying. As a longtime educational leader, I had spoken those words to others. I liked being the one who reached out in support. I enjoyed feeling confident and capable. And now, here I was, the one others believed in. It was then that I realized the importance of the "we." The plural pronoun communicated the power of the community.

We began the final climb with great care. By now it was raining steadily and the rocks grew slippery. My support system increased as others encouraged and invested in my successful ascent. Every step was planned strategically, and I was enveloped in the others' support and investment in my success. As I took the final steps, one of my class members, Mike, reached out to pull me to the peak. I slipped. He did not let go. I regained my footing, and with the help and encouragement of everyone by now, I was pulled to the top. The natural beauty was magnificent. The feeling of having arrived was exhilarating. But there are no words to describe the feeling of being there with and because of my colleagues and classmates.

The months since have turned to years, but the impact of what happened grows. As important as it is to contribute, it is equally important to receive. Generosity plays a key role in ensuring that others accomplish their goals. Investing in and strengthening others matters. And the six words—we believe you can do it—live on in my head and heart. They were important to me and have great impact when spoken to others.

Judy Wallis is a teacher, educational consultant, and lifelong learner and lives in Sugar Land, Texas.

QUIET LOYAL SUPPORT

There are times when the fullness of relationships developed in ALF can bridge divides that ideology and intellect can't. "Barbara and I had never met before ALF," says Cynthia Elsberry (ALF-Waccamaw):

> And it didn't matter that our pasts were very different or that she was African American and I was Caucasian. We were soul mates.
>
> A few months after our initial year in ALF came to a close, I was in a Board of Education meeting when a really painful incident about race came up. The conversation was anxious and fearful. Then across the room I saw Barbara sitting in the midst of my detractors. As the emotions began to peak, I looked up, our eyes met, and she gave me a warm smile. Her look signaled support and confidence in me and gave me strength. I had the strong sense that she was assuring her friends, and me, that her friend sitting at the dais at that board meeting was a good, fair person, that I would never do anything to harm or demean anyone else racially.
>
> With my confidence restored by Barbara's "message" of support, I proceeded to explain my decision with assurance.
>
> **Cynthia Elsberry is superintendent of schools in Horry County and lives in Conway, South Carolina.**

"WE NEVER REALLY DETERMINED WHO GOT IT RIGHT"

The potent linkage between primacy of relationship and genuine appreciation of diversity shines through in the story of Denise Bradley (ALF-Houston), whose year in the program came just as she was transitioning from twenty-five years as a prosecutor to a seat on the criminal district court bench. Her learning adventure began in her first class meeting when she met her "buddy" for the year:

> We came from completely opposite sides of the criminal justice arena. But true to ALF's basic approach, I got to know my buddy on a personal level before we ever discussed what goes on at the courthouse. We found out that we had several things in common. I learned that we both had family members

in law enforcement. We shared our frustration at dealing with teenagers and we both had dealt with divorce.

Our trip to Colorado really solidified the bonds and friendships that we made in ALF. It was also a perfect forum for highlighting our differences. While we had a goal to reach the top of the mountain, it was clear that the whole group couldn't make it. I immediately joined the group of five people that decided to go to the top to achieve our goal. My buddy stayed behind with the rest of the group because his sense of community was that no one should be left behind. We never really determined who got it right.

It was also on the Colorado trip that we began serious discussions about what was wrong at the courthouse. I quickly realized that to the rest of the group, I represented one of the "powerful few" while my buddy represented the voice of the "powerless masses." It gave me an opportunity to view the criminal justice system from the perspective of people who feel they aren't treated fairly.

After the Colorado trip I asked my buddy to serve as one of my grand jurors and he readily agreed. I hope it gave him a different perspective and a recognition that many of the important decisions that are made at the courthouse are made by citizens just like him. He and others encouraged me to look beyond what happens in the courtroom and into the consequences, intended and sometimes unintended, of placing an offender on probation. This was the beginning of our ALF class project.

We started by inviting the head of the probation department, probation officers, and probationers to meet with us on separate occasions. We quickly realized that many of the issues were systemic. Probationers were required to wait all day to sign up for community service, and when they reported to perform community service hours, they were often turned away because all the positions were filled by people who got in line before them. My buddy continually pointed out that I had the power to make change. I found out he was right; judges are actually in charge of the probation department, and I do have the power.

We are working together to recommend some important changes that will affect the way we deal with offenders on probation. By bringing together leaders from criminal justice, ALF fostered meaningful relationships that will have a positive impact on the way we do business at the courthouse.

Denise Bradley is the presiding judge of the 262nd Criminal District Court and lives in Houston, Texas.

TRUST SMOOTHES A TRADITIONALLY ROUGH ROAD

Over the years of her involvement in animal welfare, Kathleen Olson (ALF-Tacoma) often noticed tension between municipal animal control departments and local humane societies. That's why an experience during her ALF year was so striking.

> I had just returned from the wilderness week when contract negotiations began between the Humane Society and the local animal control jurisdictions for which we provide sheltering and adoption services. These meetings had been contentious in the past, taking several sessions to iron things out. The auditor and senior staffer with the county were both ALF senior fellows. Imagine the surprise of the other meeting participants when these two greeted me with hugs and asked about my wilderness experience. Negotiations took about ninety minutes.
>
> What was the difference? Mutual trust between ALF fellows and an honest exchange of expectations. When the city contract meeting was held a week later, negotiations took less than thirty minutes, since the lead for the city, Police Captain Mike Miller, and I were ALF classmates.

Kathleen Olson directs the Humane Society of Tacoma/ Pierce County and lives in Tacoma, Washington.

DEFUSING A NEEDLESS CRISIS

MayYing Ly (ALF-Mountain Valley) is a Hmong refugee from Laos who immigrated with her parents to the United States, along with thousands of Laotians in the aftermath of the fall of Laos to communist control in 1975. Many years later a revered leader in exile, General Vang Pao, was charged with violating the U.S. Neutrality Act because of his political activity, and brought to federal court in Sacramento for trial. This was, says MayYing, a traumatic flashback of the final evacuation days of Long Cheng, the CIA headquarters in Laos during the Vietnam Conflict where thousands were left stranded not knowing what lay ahead. Young and old were shocked by the allegations of the U.S. government. Gen. Vang Pao was considered by many as *Hmoob niam thiab Hmoob txiv,* or "Hmong mother and father," to whom many Hmong owed their lives. A massive Hmong organization emerged across the nation to rally support for the general and demand his release. Over 10,000 people were expected to demonstrate in Sacramento.

Discovering that no permit had been secured, we envisioned thousands of elderly Vang Pao followers who did not speak English getting arrested because they would not understand an order to disperse. If this happened, they could be deported for violating a federal law. It was Sunday evening, hours before the event was to begin, and we knew we had to somehow secure a permit; there was no way to stop the thousands who were already en route from all over California and the world to downtown Sacramento.

Both Sacramento City Police Chief Al Najera and Deputy Chief of Police Steve Segura were ALF senior fellows. Steve responded to my call by immediately calling the U.S. marshal, who then called me within minutes. They were thankful that we had informed them of the upcoming rally, especially with the number of people we were expecting. The marshal secured a special verbal permit from the Government Service Agency, instructing me to come downtown early the next morning to complete the paperwork. I did, and over five thousand Hmong demonstrators surrounded the courthouse and the state capitol for a peaceful rally in support of the release of the general and his alleged co-conspirators.

ALF senior fellows in our chapter continued to assist me throughout the years with the case. We had information sessions about the Hmong for all ALF members, including presentations from the police and FBI. At one point the general, who was in ill health, collapsed in jail, prompting fears of possible rioting if he died there. As a networked group, we eventually succeeded in gaining the general's release on bail. Some time later the federal case against Gen. Vang Pao and other Hmong leaders was dropped.

We can't know whether my ALF colleagues and I were instrumental in the positive outcome of this historic case in the end. But we know that in the beginning we made a huge difference, because one ALF fellow answered that critical phone call from another.

MayYing Ly is executive director of the Southeast Asian Assistance Center and lives in Sacramento, California.

A BRAVE PHONE CALL

Michele Lew (ALF-Silicon Valley) says she'd done more than her share of team-building rituals and bonding activities by the time she entered ALF. She remembers how the skepticism she brought into the room flared up when a trainer brought out a tennis ball for a well-worn exercise in group creativity. At that moment she had few expectations that the program would do much to fortify her capacity to contribute to her troubled community:

> That was a time when tensions were running high between the San Jose Police Department and ethnic communities. Community leaders pointed to disproportionate arrests of Latinos for public intoxication, as well as two separate police shootings where Vietnamese individuals were killed.
>
> During one ALF class session, I got a phone call telling me that a Vietnamese man had been beaten and stunned with a Taser gun by San Jose police officers. The incident was caught on video and was so explosive that my first reaction was fear for the safety of my community.
>
> I turned to my ALF colleagues at lunchtime for immediate help in thinking through the best way to respond. That helped me realize that though my day job had nothing to do with police/community relations, I couldn't just stand on the sidelines.
>
> About this time I saw an email from a community activist who supported the San Jose Police Department and sharply criticized community leaders objecting to police practices. Reflecting on what I was learning in ALF, I realized I needed to listen more to better understand voices like hers. Although we had never met before, I picked up the phone and called to invite her to coffee.

She was wary and didn't initially agree to a meeting. But the more we talked, the more we realized we had similar goals: a safer and inclusive San Jose with better communication among the diverse stakeholders. The phone call led to a series of community dialogues. We brought police leadership to the same circle as ethnic community residents and we started building new relationships.

Some time later, chatting with my ALF classmates over another meal, I described my disappointment at what transpired at a recent police/community dialogue, where a grieving father asked the police chief why they had to kill his son. Likely heeding his attorney's advice, the chief offered no real response. One of my ALF classmates offered a suggestion: what if the police chief and the grieving father could get in a room and just talk, without any lawyers or threats of lawsuits, and hear each other out?

Now we frequently have Dialogue on police/community issues. I'm glad that my skepticism about ALF curriculum was proven wrong.

Michele Lew is president and CEO of Asian Americans for Community Involvement and lives in Palo Alto, California.

EARNING THE BENEFIT OF THE DOUBT

Margaret Fortune (ALF-Mountain Valley) is certain that her school's impact in service to disadvantaged students was greatly amplified by the strength of an ALF relationship:

Four years ago, fed up with the glacial pace of change for students who drop out of our public schools, I decided to leave my position as education adviser to California's governor. I was quietly beginning to lose hope that the state would ever figure out how to educate children to a level of excellence, a frightening prospect for students who depend on public institutions for a viable future.

I left in order to open schools for African American children, the lowest-performing group of students in California. I figured going to a great school, beginning with kindergarten, could be a game-changer, especially for the boys who are statistically more likely to go to jail than to college. I would take the small educational nonprofit for training teachers that my parents ran for decades and reinvent it to open charter schools.

While I was packing up my boxes in the Governor's Office, I received a phone call from the American Leadership Forum. I was told that ALF had been following my career and wanted me to join its next class. As it turns out, that phone call was the turning point that made my leap of faith pay off. Through ALF I focused on building relationships with people from my region who care deeply about stewardship.

The ALF tie opened up doors and ears to what we wanted to do. My organization's bank of twenty years wouldn't grant us a loan to convert an abandoned shopping mall into a school. We were then turned down by a local community bank. Then I learned that the president of the community bank was an ALF senior fellow. I met with him directly and told him my story. ALF won me the benefit of the doubt with him. He reversed his staff's decision and gave us the loan that enabled us to build our first school.

Now, several years later, we've opened three schools serving nine hundred students. We've been authorized to open seven more, all focused on the achievement and success of African American children. ALF matured me to fully engage in that objective. It also won me a set of allies who believe in me as much as my cause.

Margaret Fortune is president and CEO of Fortune School and lives in Sacramento, California.

"…BUT LET'S FIGURE OUT ANOTHER WAY"

Jonathan Kresken was deeply involved in the founding of ALF's Waccamaw region chapter. He discovered that the civic benefits generated by well-developed relationships may not unfold right away. Patience is still a virtue.

Jonathan tells of an encounter between two classmates, the manager of the local bus system and a county councilor, who had not worked well together before their year in ALF. The bus manager appeared before the county council for additional funding during a very tight budget period. People in attendance were struck by the warmth they showed to each other, and the thoughtful quality of the policy conversation—which resulted in the council's refusal of the funding request. "But though they told him 'no' at that meeting," says Jonathan,

> an important relationship existed, and with it some shared commitment to achieve the goal at hand, which they did down the line. He got the requested funding later. That's what's important. There's a listening with respect, which doesn't mean you always get what you want, or get agreement. What you get is caring, and interest that says, "this won't work, but let's figure out another way to get the job done."

Jonathan Kresken is an attorney and lives in Myrtle Beach, South Carolina.

CHAPTER 5:
APPRECIATION, EXPLORATION, AND INCLUSION OF DIVERSITY

*"Nobody successfully maneuvers today's world
ignoring the diversity of people all around them.
Try that and you're throwing yourself off a cliff."*

—Cathy Mincberg, ALF-Houston

THE EXTRAORDINARY VALUE of human diversity still escapes widespread understanding. Some think its importance is overstated and some think the attention paid to it is a bow to political correctness. Its meaning can also be falsely relegated to only obvious attributes: race, color, national origin, gender, age, economic status, and sexual orientation. There is less awareness of our diversity in cultural attitudes, in the way we receive and filter information, and in the ways in which we process information to formulate opinions and make decisions.

ALF grapples with these complexities to help participants deepen their understanding and appreciation of diversity. For most fellows this value carries a moral component that relates to respect and human dignity. But beyond that lies recognition of the practical realities of contemporary life. Inclusion of diversity is not a feel-good ritual; it is a prerequisite to leadership that is vibrant and adaptable enough to ably serve complex, increasingly diverse communities.

"We are hampered by significant society divisions," says Luther Jackson (ALF-Silicon Valley),

> including race, gender, sexual orientation, economic status, and more. They make it difficult to achieve the community solidarity demanded for the New Economy. And yet, just the ability to talk honestly about racial issues remains elusive. Without greater understanding and recognition of our common humanity we cannot move forward. Through ALF we have the tools and the committed relationships of our networks needed to bring Silicon Valley, and ultimately our country, to a more cohesive and productive state. Leave diverse voices off to the side these days and you will lose pieces of the puzzle you may never recover. You can think of it as the "resource inefficiency of exclusion."

At the root of the appreciation of diversity is a basic belief that every individual's perceptions and cognitive processes have limitations; in the words of a Houston senior fellow, "The we will always be smarter than the me."

Bringing obvious diversity to the table has another advantage: when not everyone looks and sounds more or less the same, members of the group are less vulnerable to a mistaken belief that their thinking is more or less the same. That careless assumption can plant the seed for muddled and frustrating conflict down the line.

> *"The leadership task—indeed the task of every citizen—is to bring the gifts of those on the margin into the center."*
>
> **—Peter Block,** *Community*

"And if thinking in the group *is* in fact the same," says Chris Block, CEO of the Silicon Valley chapter, then "we continue to have the same people, proposing the same solutions in the same way—everyone playing their particular parts, in front of the same audiences leading to the same resolutions. When the community is diverse and the community is in the room and a true Dialogue ensues, then we are going to create new and innovative solutions, even when the challenges are very complex. Furthermore, relationships are formed that allow these solutions to actually be implemented."

RECONCILING OLD WOUNDS

"I had always considered myself not prejudiced, but I'd had little actual exposure to people of color," says Wayne Clark (ALF-Oregon), who moved west recently from "a very white place"—the state of Maine. It didn't take long, he says,

> "Every single year I hear folks say 'I never hang out with people like you, and I love it. I would never do this on my own, and to make the kind of difference I want to make, I have to.'"
>
> —Bill Proudman, facilitator

to understand just how privileged my white male middle-class life had been. I learned about institutionalized racism, which carries on the damage even when white people like me aren't knowingly causing it.

I'm responsible for marketing and community relations for Legacy Health, which includes Legacy Emanuel Medical Center. In the early 1970s, what was then Emanuel Hospital wanted to expand. This was the heyday of urban renewal, and the hospital's desire for expansion and the city's desire to renew formed a perfect storm that relocated the poor, mostly black residents of the neighborhood and leveled it. This had been the social and business focal point of the black community, and it was gone. Worse, the hospital never built anything on the vacant land. The gravel lot was an open sore for the black community and fueled ongoing anger and resentment.

The more I learned about how Portland in general and our predecessor hospital in particular had treated the black community, the more I felt compelled to act. But my ALF experience had taught me that I might not be in the best position to do so. I was a veteran public relations professional, but I was also a white guy from New England. I knew that I needed help from someone who knew what being black in Portland meant and who knew the community.

I called one of my ALF classmates, Jeana Woolley, and we noodled my idea of a "reconciliation" process over lunch. I ended up retaining her to help us create a process and navigate the community, starting with the people who had actually been relocated. Jeana tracked them down and invited ten of them to a "storytelling" session that began with dinner, combining what I learned were two culturally appropriate practices. We asked them to talk about the old neighborhood and the relocation, while seven of us, including the current administrator of the hospital and the system CEO, listened.

In a follow-up meeting, we shared our response to the stories and then asked for their thoughts on how we could move forward with the community respectfully and productively. We wanted to find ways to acknowledge the unfairness of what had happened and to assure them that it would not happen again. At this writing, we are still engaged in the process, but the response from our storytellers and others has been promising. Reconciliation takes time, but we're on the right path.

Wayne Clark is vice president for community relations and marketing at Legacy Health and lives in Tigard, Oregon.

FROM THE "OTHER" ACROSS THE TABLE

"In reality, we have similar challenges dressed up in very different scenarios," says Terry Cross (ALF-Oregon), a Seneca Indian who works today with other Native American communities. That was the realization he drew from extended small-group conversations he had with a corporate executive and a police chief in his class:

I had felt confident as a leader in my own field before that, but this unique opportunity confirmed that basic leadership dynamics are transferable to different contexts. I knew then that I could hold my own with leaders across a variety of sectors. Earlier moments in my ALF class had helped pave the way to this moment of clarity. In preparing for our mountain trek I shared teaching from my Seneca cultural heritage. My perspective was discussed, embraced, and put into practice.

As my confidence grew, I found new energy to tackle bigger challenges, in myself, in my organization, and in racial healing and race equity. I became a better fundraiser, no longer feeling separated by class or role. I became a better advocate, confronting injustices with new skills that allowed me to channel energy into negotiation and persuasion rather than nonproductive frustration. ALF helped me shed a one-down orientation, which I now know is a symptom of intergenerational and historical traumas shared by many of my culture.

I became a better facilitator of "courageous conversations." I became much more direct than before, learning to compassionately push others to take risks to understand and get what they most want. The experience taught me that even the person who is the most different from you has something to teach you. Oddly enough, my buddy, a county commissioner whose politics were the polar opposite of mine, became my close confidant. I came to understand that the "other" across the table, no matter how different from me, can help me reach insights I could not find alone. I learned to appreciate the integrity of a leader even if I did not agree with his or her position. Before this experience I never would have had the *authority of voice* to do that.

Terry Cross is executive director of the National Indian Child Welfare Association and lives in Portland, Oregon.

BEYOND LISTENING TO HEARING

Almost by definition, a genuinely diverse community will have friction points as it grows and changes. Those who work in social services have particular need for tools to manage these rough patches. Though Pamela Jefsen (ALF-Charlotte) was a seasoned professional when she entered ALF, she credits the program with attuning her senses to the needs of people who stood in opposition to a project important to her:

> I am executive director of an organization that develops apartment communities for people who are disabled and formerly homeless. We planned a project in a diverse, eclectic, urban neighborhood, and the neighbors were not happy. We told them that we would keep having community meetings until everyone's questions had been answered.
>
> In a typical meeting I was answering questions for two or three hours at a time. Some of the questions held anger and were not based on facts. Drawing on my ALF work, I was able to stay focused on the perspectives of the people I was talking to. I tried to put myself in the place of the people in

the neighborhood—to understand their fears, their concern for their homes and families. I considered my reality—knowing our residents, knowing them as people—different from the reality of the neighbors who may only have knowledge of the negative stereotypes. Most of the neighbors did come around and, judging from feedback I received, felt heard even if they disagreed with me.

There was a couple at one meeting who had a three-year-old daughter named Holly. Holly's father was clearly agitated by the idea of having formerly homeless and disabled people (particularly men) nearby. At one point he asked me, "Why do you think it is a good idea to bring these people who have been homeless and are addicted to drugs into a facility across the street when they may hurt our children?"

I started my answer with, "What you need to know is …" and instantly realized that those words would likely offend and further rile him up. So I stopped, took a deep breath, apologized, and started again with, "What I have learned as a result of my experience is …" Later on in the meeting the same man leaned forward, pushed his finger toward my face, and said, "If something happens to my Holly it will be all your fault and then what will you do?" I was able to hear his fear and stay calm rather than feel defensive. I simply said to him, "If my experience told me that our residents would be a danger to children, I would not be able to do this work."

I don't know how much of an impact our conversation had on this father. I did see him at another meeting, where he appeared calm rather than angry.

Pamela Jefsen is executive director of Supportive Housing Communities and McCreesh Place and lives in Charlotte, North Carolina.

A LIFELONG PURSUIT

And for anyone who doubts that exploration of diversity is a lifelong pursuit, there is an instructive memory from Anne Udall (ALF-Oregon and former ALF Director, Charlotte Region) who still remembers a class session on systems where the facilitator made the comment that poor parents don't care as much about their children's education as middle class and wealthy parents:

I have spent years leading ALF Programs and was now a fellow in a class, and I still didn't hear that comment in the same way a number of the people did in the room. As a woman of privilege in both my ethnicity and class, it still took me longer than I would care to admit to hear the comment as an insult to all parents. It took an African American woman in the room to challenge the stereotype the facilitator had stated. Once again, I realized how I have to be vigilant in understanding how my upbringing creates perspectives that can create blind spots. My relationships with ALFers who see and experience the world differently than I do is a gift. I am less likely to feel guilt and more likely to own my stuff, and work at being more aware the next time (and there is always a next time!).

CHAPTER 6:
DIALOGUE AND COLLABORATION

*"When most oarsmen talked about their perfect moment in a boat,
they referred not so much to winning a race, as to the feel of the boat,
all eight oars in the water together, the synchronization almost perfect.
In moments like these, the boat seemed to lift right out of the water.
Oarsmen called that the moment of swing."*

—David Halberstam, *The Amateurs*

WHEN THE VALUES of personal relationship and valuing diversity are genuinely embraced, the more *operational* value of Dialogue and collaboration readily follows.

Because it is such a powerful practice, Dialogue can readily be seen as a means to an end, a powerful tool to build capacity for collaboration. But many ALF senior fellows have come to value it highly in its own right. Its deepening impact within the organization seemed to surprise even Joseph Jaworski, who writes in *Synchronicity* that class members time and time again reported deep personal benefit from the ongoing Dialogue that was sustained over the course of the year:

> When a particular Dialogue was "completed" it was not over.
> Dialogue was not a single circumstance in the program, but
> turned out to be a way of life with the fellows—a way of life
> to which they became committed. It had a transformational
> effect upon many of the people. Repeatedly, fellows would

refer to the "mysterious power of the collective" they would experience.

Jaworski began sensing this power with one of the earliest readings of his personal quest, *The Servant as Leader*, where Robert Greenleaf poses an evocative question:

> Why is there so little listening? … Part of it, I believe, with those who lead, is that the usual leader in the face of a difficulty tends to react by trying to find someone else on whom to pin the problem, rather than by automatically responding: "I have a problem. What is it? What can I do about my problem?" The sensible person who takes the latter course will probably react by listening, and somebody in the situation is likely to say what the problem is and what should be done about it. Or enough will be heard that there will be an intuitive insight that resolves it. …True listening builds strength in other people.

With the development of Dialogue, David Bohm provided a system and integrated methodology for listening at the level that Greenleaf envisioned. Bohm's remarkable contribution was to extend his work in quantum physics, and the empirical indications of the unity of physical phenomena, into the human realm as a useful example of systems thinking. Jaworski includes a passage of Bohm's work in *Synchronicity* to suggest this principle's application to human communications:

> *"The whole already exists; it's just that we're locked in a frame of reference that keeps us from perceiving it."*
>
> **—Joseph Jaworski,** *Synchronicity*

> At present, people create barriers between each other by their fragmentary thought. Each one operates separately. When these barriers have dissolved, then there arises one mind, where they are all one unit, but each person also retains his or her own individual awareness. That one mind will still exist even when they separate, and when they come together, it will be as if they hadn't separated. It's actually a single intelligence that works with people who are moving in relationship with one another. Cues that pass from one to the other are being

picked up with the same awareness, just as we pick up cues in riding bicycles or skiing. Therefore, these people are all really one. The separation between them is not blocking. They are all pulling together. If you had a number of people who really pulled together and worked together in this way, it would be remarkable. They would stand out so much that everyone would know they were different.

Skilled practitioners of Dialogue say they have cultivated a firm sense of when their individual contribution to the discussion is being called forth by a collective presence. Short of that, there is often an enhanced willingness to examine whether one's intention in speaking has more to do with personal needs or service to the success and well-being of the group.

> *"Sometimes the most valuable sound in the room is silence."*
> **—Lynn Cunningham Brown, ALF-Houston**

THE LADDER OF INFERENCE

Dialogue practitioners have developed a number of tools over the years that can help remove barriers to quality listening and understanding. One is the Ladder of Inference, developed by former Harvard Business Professor Chris Argyris, a visual model that offers insight into common ways of perceiving and processing information. We work our way up the ladder, beginning at the bottom rung:

1. We take in objectively observable data, that which can be perceived by our five senses.

2. We filter that data, allowing some to pass to the conscious part of our mind and excluding others.

3. We make assumptions based on the selected data.

4. We come to conclusions shaped by those assumptions. The conclusions are the building blocks of our beliefs about the world, and our beliefs drive the actions we take.

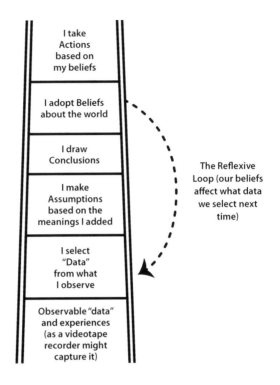

The Reflexive Loop (our beliefs affect what data we select next time)

From *The Fifth Discipline Fieldbook*, Peter M. Senge (1994)

The "reflexive loop" is the mechanism that can compromise our clarity and distort our understanding of events and people around us. In this loop our beliefs largely determine which of the available data passes through to our conscious mind, to then drive more assumptions that are likely to confirm rather than challenge preexisting beliefs. This cognitive sequence, so ingrained and habitual as to be invisible to most of us, can decisively compromise collaboration and other interpersonal activity. Dialogue practice brings it to light.

A picture of the ladder is sometimes posted prominently in the room for reference when participants feel "stuck." The practice of locating the dynamic of the present moment on the ladder and then dropping down one or more rungs can realign the group and deepen awareness of the source of clashing perceptions that block understanding.

This dynamic power of Dialogue dovetails with the emphasis Peter Block places on intentional community gatherings. In *Community* he writes:

> Every meeting or special event is that place where context can be shifted, relatedness can be built, and new conversation can be introduced. The times that we gather are when we draw conclusions about what kind of community we live in.
>
> We change the world one room at a time.

THE FOUR-PLAYER MODEL

ALF frequently makes use of David Kantor's Four-Player Dialogue Model to help the class understand the dynamics of a generative dialogue and to navigate difficult topics. The model identifies four components that are needed for a successful Dialogue: move, follow, oppose and bystand. Participants in Dialogue must ensure that each of these components is present. Individuals do not take on a specific part exclusively. Rather, they are attentive to the needs of the conversation and can provide any of the four components as needed. Senior fellows, therefore, are asked to practice fulfilling each of the four roles.

1. **Move:** This is usually a statement that advocates a position. By its expression, it moves the conversation in a specific direction.

2. **Follow/Listen:** This is usually a question that follows the direction of a move. This is meant to bring out other perspectives on the move statement or to further understand the mover's perspective.

3. **Oppose:** This is usually a statement that offers a differing opinion on the move statement. This can either be a correction of fact or advocacy of a different position.

The Four-Player Model: What Does the Dialogue Need?

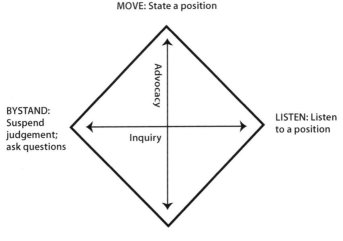

MOVE: State a position

Advocacy

BYSTAND:
Suspend
judgement;
ask questions

Inquiry

LISTEN: Listen
to a position

OPPOSE: Oppose a position

4. **Bystand:** This is usually an observation of what is happening in the group. This is used to monitor the quality of the Dialogue. For example, someone might say, "I notice that some in the group seem very emotional right now. I wonder if we need to take a moment to talk about why."

THE CHALLENGE OF COLLABORATION

Dialogue can nurture interpersonal bonds that help overcome the common obstacles to collaboration. One of those obstacles is rooted in the structure of the human brain. Studies of the brain reveal that its components—the so-called "reptilian brain" (brain stem), the "mammalian" or limbic brain, and the prefrontal cortex, unique to primates—operate quite differently.

The prefrontal cortex creates a sense of self, develops insight and empathy, and forms moral judgments. This area enables humans to pause before we act. When it is engaged and in charge, we are able to reflect, organize, be creative, think, and listen. But when we feel significant threat, our reptilian brain, the part wired to fight, flee, or freeze, hijacks our feelings and behavior. We then have less access to our "thinking" brain and therefore to our capacity for listening, learning, and constructive exchange.

When respectful, empathic relationships are developed and the importance of diversity is clear, we less frequently perceive stimuli as threats that kick-start the reptilian brain. Our capacity to listen and loosen our grip on earlier beliefs tends to expand, and the benefits of collaboration are easier to keep foremost in our thinking.

A growing body of behavioral and neurological data confirms the critical need for collaboration. Compiling the results of various studies in his 2012 book, *The Righteous Mind*, social psychologist Jonathan Haidt bluntly exposes the blind spots that hamper individual human thinking. "…each individual reasoner," he writes,

> is really good at one thing: finding evidence to support the position that he or she already holds, usually for intuitive reasons. We should not expect individuals to produce good, open-minded truth-seeking reasoning, particularly when self-interest or reputational concerns are in play. But if you put individuals together in the right way, such that some individuals can use their reasoning powers to disconfirm the claims of others, and all individuals feel some common bond or shared fate that allows them to interact civilly, you can create a group that ends up producing good reasoning as an emergent property of the social system.
>
> This is why it's so important to have intellectual and ideological diversity within any group or institution whose goal is to find truth (such as an intelligence agency or a community of scientists) or to produce good public policy (such as a legislature or advisory board).

Although the ALF experience often deepens appreciation and awareness of collaboration, it is rarely a new concept for ALF fellows. "Collaboration is the only way to accomplish big projects with various stakeholders," says Pamela Jefsen (ALF-Charlotte).

Dan Murrey (ALF-Charlotte) is CEO of one of the nation's

largest orthopedic care systems. His father was a country doctor, "completely responsible for the health care people received. That was then. With the complexity and countless dimensions of *today's* health care system, nobody can begin to pull that off alone. Unless you're Dr. Quinn, Medicine Woman on the frontier, you just can't do this by yourself."

Collaboration has more purposes than generating optimal decisions in a complex world. It can also develop capacity in organizations and communities. Jan McGowan (ALF-Oregon), who for years led a nonprofit organization helping small communities set and accomplish civic goals, sees collaboration as a step to greater achievement:

> It's essential that everyone own a piece of the project, no matter how small or unlike leadership the piece might look like. People self-select what they're good at, or feel capable of, and you grow things from there. Once they're in, they can stretch toward more leadership.

The notion of *ownership* comes up repeatedly among leaders with collaborative experience. They see it as an early-stage requirement for eventual success. As Dan Murrey says, "The degree of buy-in to decisions takes things a long way. And you rarely get much buy-in from people who aren't an important part of the process."

> *"The trouble with coercive power is that it only strengthens resistance. And, if successful, its controlling effect lasts only as long as the force is strong. It is not organic. Only persuasion and the consequent voluntary acceptance are organic."*
>
> **—Robert Greenleaf,**
> ***The Servant as Leader***

"I want every perspective and I want us to collectively decide the way forward," says Rick Little (ALF-Tacoma). "Allowing people to be part of the development leads to ownership, and ownership leads to commitment. One-off discussions or silos lead to the garbled muck that resulted from the old kids' telephone game. If there are differences, I want everyone to hear them at the same time and I want us to resolve them as a group."

For some ALF fellows, collaboration can be easier to describe and praise than practice. Many have been hard-chargers through their academic and professional lives, rewarded for individual initiative and problem solving. Some have much less patience with group process than others. You may hear them describe past ordeals in meeting rooms that sound as if they've been scarred for life.

The tension between the need for consensus and the need to finalize and implement decisions diminishes, both in frequency and intensity, when quality relationships have been developed. "Winning" on a particular decision usually doesn't carry the urgency that it does when relationships are weak and people feel a sharp need for recognition and acceptance. "Learning to live with outcomes other than what you wanted," says Laurie Jinkins (ALF-Tacoma), "is very important in the long run."

> "Leadership is the ability to reach a decision where even those who don't agree believe they had input and respect, and that the action is for the common good."
>
> **—Bill Johnston, ALF-Tacoma**

Other fellows suggest that when consensus is elevated to a stand-alone value, other group needs might be ignored. Brenda Wensil (ALF-Charlotte), working in the Office of Federal Student Aid in the U.S. Department of Education, says:

> Creating a focus around student borrowers has required bringing people together across divisions. Any one area or any one leader cannot accomplish this alone, but the value of leveraging the thinking and resources of a wider group is helping to turn the tide. In this endeavor, it has been helpful to stay clear on the distinction between collaboration and consensus building. Collaboration, in my experience, is the stronger of the two. Consensus building, while probably critical in some environments, can take far too much time and lead to less than optimal outcomes.

Some fellows, accustomed to decades of accolades as the

Smartest Guy or Gal in the Room, freely admit that embracing collaboration can be difficult. Dan Murrey, ALF-Charlotte, is comfortable with the shift. He says that being the smartest guy in the room doesn't translate to knowing the best solution in every situation. "And I might *still* think I'm the smartest guy in the room, but I'm self-assured enough that I have no need to show it. I use my smarts to try to learn from everyone else in the room. That's how I get smarter."

COLLABORATION TO TAP INTO INVALUABLE EXPERIENCE

Webb McKinney's (ALF-Silicon Valley) commitment to collaboration has long been a central thread of his work. His year in ALF was the threshold between a thirty-four year career at Hewlett-Packard and what he calls his "encore career" volunteering in the nonprofit sector:

> The experience of helping a classmate's organization expand to meet its growing needs caused me to start thinking about how the nonprofit sector could get greater benefit from all the baby boomers starting to retire from Silicon Valley companies. I met with classmate Carol Larson, president of the David and Lucile Packard Foundation, to share my thoughts on how to work with high-tech companies and nonprofits to transfer a lot more expertise.
>
> Carol was intrigued. Her foundation funded the pilot of what was to become Encore Fellowships. Ten recent retirees, several from HP, went to work halftime for a year for nonprofit organizations, who were so pleased with the quality of the help that they all asked to have a Fellow assigned to them the following year. In just four years' time we've grown that pilot into ten programs spread all over the country (one run by the ALF chapter in Sacramento) with more than two hundred Encore Fellows.
>
> One of the major things I learned from many hours of Dialogue in my ALF class is that people from the for-profit and not-for-profit worlds have very strong views about one another, and they are not all positive. We used this understanding in the design of the Encore Fellows program. We included open

discussion among the Fellows, and combined communication sessions with the Fellows and the agency directors. This turned out to be critical to the success of the program. Encore Fellows would not have come into existence without ALF.

Webb McKinney is a retired Hewlett-Packard executive and lives in Los Altos, California.

CHANGING THE TONE OF CITY GOVERNMENT

Wendy Mattson Thomas (ALF-Mountain Valley) was determined to apply what she learned in her class year to her work on the Placerville, California, city council. She says that when she was elected, her community felt estranged from the political process:

> *"The function of leadership is to produce more leaders, not more followers."*
>
> **—Ralph Nader**

> The consensus of a small, vocal, well-organized, and contentious minority was that projects were being pushed on the community that did not reflect the will of the people. Their rhetoric led to a growing mistrust of local government, and their position was to take us to court or the ballot on any issue they didn't agree with.
>
> A light switched on for me when we read Peter Block's work about the possibilities of transforming community through powerful conversations. Meeting with my ALF class monthly allowed me to hone this skill. Consequently I developed a series of Neighborhood Chats and Community Coffees that our city adopted as an ongoing program. It transformed the way we spoke to each other.
>
> At our first chat, a casually-dressed council warmly greeted incoming citizens at a table laden with flowers and refreshments. The dais was gone, and in its place were chairs placed in the round. There was no "middleman" in the room, no out-of-town consultant telling us "how to be when we grew up." There was the council and city staff (who had volunteered their time to be there) in the midst of community members having a conversation.
>
> After a heartfelt welcome, I named the elephant in the room—all the ways that we had been stuck in our pattern of

relating to each other—and emphasized that no topic was off the table. Then I laid out rules of Dialogue for the evening's discussion, designed to welcome diverse thought in our search for positive solutions. Then, not knowing what I was opening us up to, we began.

We asked what they liked about our community and what they didn't. We talked about the challenges we face as a city and what ideas they had for improvement. And the most amazing thing happened: the community responded. The Dialogue was warm and engaging. Even in discussing the challenges with our city, the conversation was respectful and proactive. The citizens that yelled and railed on us week after week showed up in a different manner. Citizens walked away with a new view of their local government as being responsive, approachable, and open, and we walked away encouraged and invigorated with renewed determination to lead according to our shared values.

Our council meetings now have a different tone and tenor, and the citizens who felt obliged to verbally attack us have either stopped attending or have completely changed the way they show up at our meetings. I would not have believed such a rapid and complete transformation was possible in a community had I not experienced it. I also believe that we, the elected leadership, are holding ourselves differently, more accurately reflecting the community as a whole, all because we dare to better understand each other.

Wendy Mattson Thomas is a member of the Placerville City Council and lives in Placerville, California.

A LITERAL LIFE SAVER

It's safe to say that more than a few young Texans are alive and healthy today because of the tenacious commitment of a group of Houston senior fellows. During their ALF year in the mid 1980s, the infant mortality rate in their community—12.5 per 1000 live births—was about thirty percent above the national average, and almost twice the Surgeon General's Year 2000 goal of 6.5.

Lan Bentsen (ALF-Houston) knew that his community could do better. From his time as a March of Dimes volunteer he understood that the failure of responsible agencies to coordinate their services was a major cause of the problem. He describes how mundane missteps often led to terrible outcomes:

A high-risk pregnancy patient diagnosed at a city clinic would be handed her records and told to go make an appointment with the county hospital. If she were, say, a 15-year-old, she would likely never get there for any number of reasons—fear, loss of records, inability to get an appointment after working hours, lack of bilingual operators, lack of a "hot line"—all manageable circumstances, assuming cooperation. Left alone, her high-risk conditions prevailed until she went into labor, too often with disastrous results.

ALF Houston Class 3 offered to intervene. We felt a community-wide effort would be required to overcome the inertia of the two agencies. Because the subject of prenatal care in those days had become linked with extenuating social issues, we knew all parties that could "veto" the effort had to be involved. In particular, the March of Dimes and the faith community had to come to the table.

To broaden the collaboration, the ALF class members recruited thirty other community organizations with a range of views on health issues. A mission statement was defined, step by laborious step. Our ALF training had taught us that no step could be taken unless all parties agreed. Confidence grew. Respect for values was developed. Misconceptions were identified and clarified. The ALF collaboration approached the city and the county with a request to implement the changes. All leaders agreed that the steps and recommendations were reasonable and desirable.

But somehow nothing seemed to change.

The ALF collaboration then turned to the media, which was suitably impressed with the breadth and depth of the collaboration and its mission. Media cameras entered the clinics asking to see the (nonexistent) multilingual hot-lines for making appointments. The newspaper tracked on the front page how long it took to get an appointment with the county system for high-risk city pregnancies. The television stations visited the "baby cemetery." The public pressure was unrelenting.

Things changed fast at that point. Systems were integrated

quickly, because they had already been designed and funded. Clinics opened on evenings and weekends. Patient records were hand-delivered and appointment reminders were sent to patients. The bus system offered free passes. And the high-risk city pregnancies began to get first-trimester care.

Within three years, infant deaths dropped from six hundred to three hundred per year in the city and county, even as the local birthrate continued to increase dramatically. Houston achieved its year 2000 Surgeon General goal of 6.5 infant deaths per 1000 live births in five years, ten years ahead of schedule.

As it happened, the lieutenant governor of Texas was a Houston resident and saw this unfold. He convened the Select Committee on Medicaid and Family Services and recruited ALF class members to serve on it and make recommendations to the state. The Maternal Infant Health Improvement Act was subsequently submitted to the Texas Legislature.

Over the next five years infant mortality incidence in Texas declined from 3,000 to 2,000 deaths. The state's infant mortality ranking improved from 49th to 26th, a ranking it continues to hold more than twenty years later.

Lan Bentsen is a civic entrepreneur and lives in Houston, Texas.

PRIDE IN PLACE

Connie Martinez (ALF-Silicon Valley) relied on collaboration to help raise her city's cultural and aesthetic quality of life—the visible *exterior* of community—towards the same level as its intellectual and scientific accomplishments:

Although globally acclaimed for technology and innovation, Silicon Valley tends to "live in its head" without manifesting its creativity and innovation in the physical realm where we actually live, work, and raise our families. With that end in mind, a growing leadership network launched a series of initiatives, anchored in arts and urban design, as strategies for community building and place-making.

Over an eight-year period, the collaborative work of sixty-five ALF senior fellows, more than a hundred organizations, and four thousand local people has made a huge difference. Improvements to downtown San Jose and the San Jose airport have been completed and more are under way. A new urban plaza or "outdoor living room" for the arts is under construction. An urban market has opened. A first-ever regional marketing campaign for the arts, with a technology platform called LiveSV focused on cultural engagement, is in place. A failed cultural facility in east San Jose has transformed into the successful School of Arts and Culture and multicultural gathering space. A children's creativity initiative serving tens of thousands of children and youth is in its incubation phase. The list of accomplishments is broad and deep and continues to grow.

None of this would have happened the way it happened, and as swiftly as it happened, without the ALF network. The network brought courage, comfort, and access to resources, all anchored in a culture of trust, respect, and possibility—the culture of ALF.

Connie Martinez is CEO of Silicon Valley Creates and lives in San Jose, California.

A POWERFUL TOOL FOR COLLABORATION

David Lowe's (ALF-Mountain Valley) professional work offers a distinctively powerful community tool. He says that shortly after taking the helm of Sacramento's public television station, he was feeling discouraged about the prospects of producing a local weekly series, an important goal for anyone in his position. "There was just no funding for it," he says. Then he chose to let go of his notion of what couldn't be done:

> I made the shift to wonder, "How can we produce a series with no funding?" The answer wasn't going to be in cutting corners. The staff had to be talented, the studio set professional, and the host worthy of a national stage.
>
> At about that time I heard from senior fellow Scott Syphax, who wanted to share his idea for a new series. I told him that I loved the idea, partly because it was mine. When it was clear we were not only on the same page but also the same sentence, I asked, "Are you telling me you want to be the host?" Knowing our zero budget, he agreed to serve as our volunteer host.
>
> Why was I so confident we could produce this new series? Because I knew my ALF senior fellows would be instrumental

in surfacing topics and being guests. Soon we formalized an arrangement for ALF to be our editorial partner for one episode each month.

Now our Emmy award-winning Studio Sacramento has more programs in the works that will engage our community in meaningful dialogue and serve as a launching point for conversation beyond the broadcast.

David Lowe is president and general manager of PBS station KVIE in Sacramento and lives in Elk Grove, California.

PUSHING THE "SEND" BUTTON

It was during a quiet moment at his desk, his finger hovering over his computer keyboard, that Luther Jackson (ALF-Silicon Valley) realized how deeply the dynamics that motivate his work had shifted. He credits his Dialogue experience in ALF for the change:

> To be in Dialogue is to be open to, and even welcome, new ideas and concepts that have the potential to challenge deeply held beliefs and transform worldviews. But I've learned that the road to Dialogue is rarely straight or smooth.
>
> Recently I had the Herculean task of crafting a grant application from the goals and perspectives of multiple partners from three regions of the country. We were running up against a tight deadline and I had to cobble together the first draft of a complex concept that was not yet fully formed.
>
> This draft was an absolute mess. The idea of sharing it with respected colleagues was terrifying. Although I said I was looking for their honest comments, this was one of those occasions when I was feeling particularly insecure. What I wanted, even needed, was their validation. I wanted them to tell me how much they loved my work ("Best draft ever!" "Worthy of an award!") and how much they appreciate me.
>
> I was able to push the *send* button on my computer only because I recognized, almost through an out-of-body experience, where I was getting stuck. My Dialogue skills gave me the clarity to know that my needs for validation and praise were threatening to sabotage the task at hand. That's part of the beauty of Dialogue. You gain the self-awareness that enables you to recognize your personal barriers, and can

change course to move towards more inclusion, innovation, and community solidarity.

Luther Jackson is program manager for NOVA Workforce Services in Sunnyvale and lives in San Jose, California.

A PLACE TO LISTEN

Flip Hassett's (ALF-Great Valley) dream was to create a "Listening Center," a physical space to incubate all kinds of collaboration in his community. He discovered that it could only come into being through a collaboration:

> Because grants to support physical facilities are rare, my biggest hurdle was assembling the infrastructure to form the space; computers, media and video equipment, and the list went on. My classmate Kathy Halsey of AT&T came to the rescue. She agreed that asking the right questions, convening people, and discussing our passions and commitments were critical if our region was to be successful (we should actually expand that concept to our nation and the world, but one step at a time!).
>
> Kathy found financial support for space. The room was soon accommodating city and county officials, faith-based groups, neighborhoods, nonprofit organizations—sometimes all at the same time. Well over a thousand different folks have spent countless hours in meaningful dialogue in our Listening Center, and it's starting to make a difference.
>
> For the elected officials, it has relaxed the focus to come up with solutions. For them to just listen and participate with others for potential solutions and ideas has really been helpful; they don't get blamed and they don't have to show others that they have all the answers.
>
> The following year other ideas emerged in the Listening Center through conversations with youth about the lack of job opportunities in our community. The concept of a micro-business incubator was born, with the key participation of ALF senior fellow Oscar Cabello from Wells Fargo. Oscar's passion is community and economic development in central California. We clicked almost immediately. Together we have initiated a task force, funded through Oscar's work,

aiming to bring different organizations together to encourage young entrepreneurs to create their own businesses and then mentoring them through the first five years. It is the first time I've seen people from multiple organizations really get excited about working together.

Flip Hassett is executive director of United Way of Merced County and lives in Merced, California.

OVERCOMING INSTITUTIONAL MISTRUST

The world of labor relations can be a hard place to nurture the sense of common purpose vital to collaboration. Those at the bargaining table are often swimming against a current of suspicion and resentments long harbored by people they represent. Pat Kiley (ALF-Houston) works in that pressurized world. He offered an example of how relationships forged in his class have contributed to his success:

> One of my classmates was Richard Shaw, secretary-treasurer of the Harris County AFL-CIO Council. His organization covers several unions with which I negotiated each year on behalf of a group of contractors. In typical ALF pairing fashion, Richard and I wound up roommates for the wilderness experience. The whole ALF program builds trust, but rooming together adds an extra dimension.
>
> The issue we came to tackle was Houston's Prevailing Wage Ordinance, which requires the city to specify a wage rate for each craft worker classification. All contractors working on city projects must pay the specified rate. This is an emotionally charged issue, particularly here in Texas where most contractors operate "open shop" (nonunion). The true prevailing wage rate is somewhere between the wages agreed to in the union contracts and the lower rates usually paid to the open-shop workers.
>
> When the city chooses to update its rates, it causes heartburn for contractors because they think the unions will get their contract rates approved through political influence with the city council. Both sides bombard council members. Updates to the ordinances get tabled for as long as possible and tempers flare in the union council or contractor committee meetings.

This was the environment that caused Richard and me to get busy. The administration of Mayor Lee Brown (another senior fellow) and the city council ran out of time. They had to act at the next meeting. Realizing that Shaw and I represented the two sides involved, a city staffer told Richard, "If you and Kiley can agree on the rates, we'll specify them and trust you to sell them."

Based on our relationship from ALF, we met in total trust of each other's motives, negotiated a realistic structure that council approved, and sold it to our communities. This was a perfect example of how ALF "strengthens leaders to serve the public good."

Pat Kiley is owner of Kiley Advisers and former chief executive staff for AGC Houston and lives in Houston, Texas.

PUSHING BACK AGAINST HATE

Dennis Morrow (ALF-Oregon) recounts "an optimistic dream springing from a somber reality." His class was stunned during its program year when a group of skinheads with baseball bats bludgeoned to death Mulugeta Seraw, an Ethiopian student, on the streets of Portland. The story received international attention and sparked huge reactions in the Northwest, including painfully honest dialogue in Dennis' class, which was already trying to grapple with racial tension. "Some in our class," says Dennis, "were shocked when their peers admitted they would not feel safe traveling alone in Oregon."

The dialogue produced a commitment to undertake a class project that would impact the hatred and bigotry that precipitated this tragedy. Class members found a template in a California summer program called Brotherhood-Sisterhood Camp, which many years earlier had imprinted one fellow with a deep and compassionate sensibility about prejudice and acceptance. "With no experience organizing anything remotely resembling a diversity-focused summer camp for teenagers," says Dennis,

we created a project intended to last for three years. Instead, Camp Odyssey ran for twelve, changing the lives of over a thousand youth and adults from every ethnic, socioeconomic, and geographic background in the Pacific Northwest.

But as recent FBI statistics showed that hate crimes are on the rise locally and nationally, the alumni and supporters recognized that the problem had not been contained. So in 2010, twenty years after they attended the camp as teenagers, some of the earliest Odyssey campers came together to resurrect the program. They wanted the next generation to have the same opportunity they'd had as teens.

Joined by several original camp founders and senior fellows, these alumni relaunched Camp Odyssey in 2011. Since its revival, eighty-four youths from around the state have had an experience of a lifetime and returned home to thirty high schools, yielding a potential for impacting up to 20,000 youth in these schools. The dream of Oregon ALF Class 3, updated and refined, is once again stimulating honest conversation across the state of Oregon.

I always enjoy telling people that our class was the first (and perhaps only) class that climbed to the top of the wrong mountain. But out of our experience came what might be the longest-lived of all ALF projects. This shows that it's not where you're going that's important, but who you are with and how you get there. And isn't that the real message and value of ALF?

Dennis Morrow is executive director of Janus Youth Programs and lives in Portland, Oregon.

CHAPTER 7:
SERVICE TO THE COMMON GOOD

"There are no passengers on spaceship earth. We are all crew."

—Marshall McLuhan

THE DEFINING PHRASE that ALF stamps on much of its written material is simple: *Joining and strengthening leaders to better serve the public good* (in practice, senior fellows more often use the phrase "common good"). Is "the common good" too amorphous or subjective to be a useful beacon for civic leadership? No. But it needs rigorous inquiry if it is to have enough meaning to guide the work. The comments of Oregon Chapter director Robin Teater offer useful context:

> No one who works with the kind of range and diversity of leaders that ALF consciously incorporates into its program believes that all come into this space agreeing on what, precisely, the "common good" is. It is important to acknowledge that the common good is not simply "what the majority thinks is good." An ordinary calculator can determine that. As majorities shift, whether in their political, social, demographic, or other dimensions, this simplistic definition of what constitutes the common good will shift in tandem.
>
> The obvious question before us as leaders in rapidly changing, infinitely diverse, staggeringly complex yet increasingly interrelated communities is this: How do we agree on what matters to us? But more probing suggests

that this might not be the most powerful question, because the most important goals and values among even a diverse population are remarkably similar. Do a values clarification exercise among twenty random people and it is a good bet there will be surprising consistency among the top three or four values; they will relate to family, health and well-being, peace and relative prosperity. The deeper question may well be the one that naturally follows: *How do we agree on the best way to achieve those things that matter most to us?*

The transcendent task of modern-day leadership is to develop the social capital that inspires people to expand their sense of self-interest to include their community. It requires a range of skills and attitudes that rarely make it to a list of top ten leadership traits in typical authority-based leadership models.

Far from arriving as a rescuer of communities or organizations, leaders must arrive as learners, healers, and facilitators of relationships. What they must bring are often considered the "soft" skills of leadership, sometimes dismissed as touchy-feely or just plain unnecessary. But we have discovered that before the hard or technical skills of leadership and problem solving can be effectively engaged, the soft skills must till the soil.... It serves the modern-day leader well to understand that the "soft" stuff of leadership *is* the hard stuff.

Thus it is precisely here where ALF's work begins.

NETWORKED LEADERSHIP

It would be difficult to measure ALF's role in expanding service to the common good in its home communities. While every chapter could list many of their class projects over the years, those represent only the most structured and monitored part of the picture. Much more widespread, and probably more impactful, is the sum of comparatively spontaneous collaborations between classmates, and often among fellows

"Water is fluid, soft, and yielding. But water will wear away rock, which is rigid and cannot yield. As a rule, whatever is fluid, soft, and yielding will overcome whatever is rigid and hard. This is another paradox: what is soft is strong."

—Lao-Tzu (600 B.C.)

from different classes and chapters. Participants come to think of the senior fellow network as an extraordinarily valuable resource.

The contacts they initiate within that network are never "cold calls." The ALF connection—either a significant friendship, a more casual acquaintance, or just the unspoken awareness of a yearlong set of profound experiences held in common, even among those who have never met—makes it probable that the person called will be happy to hear from the caller.

"When I need help with something," says Cathy Mincberg (ALF-Houston), "I usually ask, 'Who in ALF can help me solve this problem?' I almost always find the right person, and they almost always want to help."

Robbie Howell, director of ALF's Charlotte chapter, recalls receiving an email from a senior fellow who graduated six years before, who had just been appointed to a board in her county. She was looking for support from senior fellows in the same field. Robbie sent her contact information for three fellows, two of whom the senior fellow didn't know. "To me this is an example of ALF's power in the region," says Robbie. "These events happen every day, and I'm so used to them that I forget about them."

The result frequently affects the community in substantial ways. Luther Jackson (ALF-Silicon Valley) says, "I'll pick up the paper and see an initiative, and immediately a light bulb goes on in my

"No matter what you think you love and are committed to, once you hear of the other issues in the community your whole world opens and you start to think of whom you could connect, what influence you have in the community and how you can help foster whatever is needed to make the changes happen".
—Dorothy Gibbons, ALF-Houston

"An amazing thing about ALF is that when you get a message or call from a senior fellow, whether you know them or not, you respond, as do most other senior fellows."
—Linda Gold, ALF-Silicon Valley

head. I know how that came about—it's because so-and-so and so-and-so were in the same class together."

FOSTERING A NEW CULTURE OF GIVING

Kirk Hanson (ALF-Silicon Valley) and a group of senior fellows from the corporate sector were concerned that the new generation of Silicon Valley leaders might not show a level of commitment to the common good comparable to that of David Packard, Bill Hewlett and other pioneers of the high tech industry. They devised a high-leverage approach for upgrading corporate philanthropy in their community.

Senior fellow and venture capitalist Gib Myers developed a proposal for the Entrepreneurs' Foundation (EF), an organization that would encourage entrepreneurs to incorporate philanthropy into their start-ups from inception and assist them in instituting best practices:

> The EF model evolved rapidly to provide hands-on help to early-stage companies that wanted to begin significant community involvement sooner rather than later. They organized training sessions for small companies on corporate responsibility and provided extensive one-on-one consulting to help companies launch their efforts. The foundation later created an awards program to honor the most engaged companies.
>
> In 2007 EF started consulting with more mature companies—HP, eBay, Google, and others—that wanted to have greater social impact. EF's forums and conferences became thought-leadership platforms, and EF's website became a self-service resource center for any company, any time.
>
> Over time almost six hundred individual venture capitalists and nearly three hundred companies have committed to EF and participated in its activities. These efforts helped create a culture in Silicon Valley and in entrepreneurial centers around the world that places community engagement at the heart of start-up companies.
>
> **Kirk Hanson is executive director of the Markkula Center for Applied Ethics at Santa Clara University and lives in Los Altos, California.**

TURNING AROUND A ROUGH DOWNTOWN

"The heart of my city was being taken over by gang members," says Marcia Moe (ALF-Tacoma), whose daily walk to work took her through a deteriorating downtown. She especially remembers a day when she found herself two feet away from a drug deal as she entered her office building:

I sat at my desk with a heavy heart. What could one person do to change the streets of our city?

I told my ALF class that I was going to start a farmers market in downtown Tacoma. This was many years before markets like these became popular. My goal was to fill the streets with people and positive activities and drive out gang members and drug dealers. The wife of an ALF classmate joined my journey.

Local business people were not exactly enthusiastic. "We've tried that before and it didn't work," they told me. "Workers will not come out of their buildings during the day." "Nobody will come into downtown Tacoma to shop." "I won't do anything to hurt your project, but I won't do anything to help it either." Those who owned businesses along the street that would be closed four hours each market day went to the city en masse to protest. "Business is hard enough," they cried. "If you don't allow people to park in front of our shops, we'll go out of business!"

The day of the first farmers market dawned with blue skies and bright sunshine. As we stood on the corner at the entrance to the market, our hearts soared. A few people were actually coming out of their offices and heading for the market. Then the floodgates opened. Shoppers by the hundreds filled the streets and sidewalks heading for the market. A local baker brought forty loaves of bread for her booth; they were gone in ten minutes! Shoppers were delighted with the bargains and vendors were thrilled. Even the businesses without their parking spots were elated as their shops filled with customers.

That was over twenty years ago. Today Tacoma Farmers Market is one of the largest day markets in Washington state. With shoppers flocking to purchase beautiful fruit and vegetables, colorful bouquets and handmade crafts, Tacoma Farmers Market has contributed to the turnaround of downtown Tacoma.

Marcia Moe, a former ALF executive director, works with private foundations and lives in Tacoma, Washington.

INTEGRATING A FRACTURED SYSTEM

Mike Ziegler's (ALF-Mountain Valley) class was galvanized by a speaker from the Annie E. Casey Foundation, who made vivid the world of disadvantaged children:

> I came away believing that we as a society should be ashamed of our lack of commitment to these young individuals. To be sure, good people and programs existed even then. But for the most part young adults were emancipating out of the foster care system at high school graduation or age eighteen to the streets without support. Within five years most were homeless, imprisoned, or dead.
>
> Our class proceeded to cobble together a program from a highly disjointed system with limited funding. Today at PRIDE Industries we partner with several organizations to serve foster and at-risk youth, providing employment skills training, linkages to educational services, marketable work experience, and individualized support to secure stable employment and build a self-sufficient life.
>
> This measurable and meaningful difference is a direct result of my experience with ALF. The leadership skills we gained, as well as the exposure to such a wealth of diversity, helped bring together people committed to making their communities—and the world—a better place to be. That's pretty powerful stuff if you ask me.

Michael Ziegler is president/CEO of PRIDE Industries and lives in Auburn, California.

FACILITATING ACCESS TO THE COURTS

Chris Bragg (ALF-Charlotte) believes that his year in the program nudged him to consider more deeply the essence of his responsibility and purpose as a judge:

> As judges do on a daily basis throughout our country, I could

listen to a case, enter a ruling, and move to the next case. That's the job I was elected to do. But judges are the leaders of the court system, and as such I believe we have a greater duty and responsibility to see that justice is dispensed fairly and impartially and that all citizens regardless of socioeconomic status have access to the courts. Outside of the courtroom, judges can have a powerful and positive impact on advocating and creating programs and policies that benefit attorneys, clerks of court, and more importantly the citizens who appear before the court.

ALF strengthened and sharpened my skills. I find that I am open to dialogue, even when I firmly disagree with what I am hearing. I actually listen to what is being said without trying to interject and immediately solve the problem. In revamping our local court rules, I was tasked with seeking consensus from parties with different points of view and agendas. Working together over time to establish an environment of trust and respect for one another, we were able to adopt new rules that benefited those within the court system while serving clients as well.

Chris Bragg is a superior court judge and lives in Monroe, North Carolina.

CHAPTER 8:
INNER REFLECTION AND
PERSONAL GROWTH

*"At this time in history, we are to take nothing personally.
Least of all ourselves. For the moment that we do, our
spiritual growth and journey comes to a halt."*

—from The Hopi Elders Speak

THE FOUR VALUES we've now explored seem positive and reasonable to most people. This gives rise to a natural question: Why aren't these values more prevalent in the world of human affairs?

The ALF theory of change holds that these values will not shape behavior in a sustained way unless they are grounded in self-awareness. By this we mean not casual or occasional reflection, but rather a level of self-awareness rooted in ongoing, disciplined observation of our thought and feeling processes, and consistent willingness to challenge our prejudgments, beliefs, and ego attachments.

This was the dispositional habitat of Robert Greenleaf, David Bohm, and others who deeply influenced Joseph Jaworski. "… the servant views any problem in the world as *in here*, inside oneself, not *out there*," Greenleaf wrote in *The Servant as Leader*. "And if a flaw in the world is to be remedied, to the servant the process of change starts *in here*, in the servant, not *out there*."

In the introduction to *Synchronicity*, Peter Senge suggests that self-awareness is a precondition for the *external* awareness intrinsic to effective action in the world:

> If we could only see reality more as it is, it would become obvious what we need to do. We wouldn't be acting out of our own histories, or our own needs, or our own purely reactive interpretations. We would see what is needed in the moment. We would do exactly what's required of us, right now, right here. This is precisely what David Bohm was talking about when he spoke of living one's life by "participating in the unfolding." You can't do that unless you can actually see what is right before you.

Jaworski's narratives in *Synchronicity* and continued in *Source* challenge readers to understand the need for self-awareness as fundamental to all change.

One common outcome of the in-here inquiry is an assumption of greater accountability for aspects and conditions of our world that we don't like. This conscious movement away from blaming and insisting on change from others is a critical threshold in personal transformation. In emphasizing powerful questions, Block speaks in *Community* to the imperative of this shift:

> Achieving accountability and commitment entails the use of questions through which, in the act of answering them, we become cocreators of the world. … Powerful questions are the ones that cause you to become an actor as soon as you answer them. You no longer have the luxury of being a spectator of whatever it is you are concerned about. Regardless of how you answer these questions, you are guilty. Guilty of having created this world. Not a pleasant thought, but the moment we accept the idea that we have created the world, we have the power to change it.

And in the words of Betty Sue Flowers, Jaworski's and Senge's collaborator in the book *Presence*, "… cultivation, 'becoming a real human being,' really is the primary leadership issue of our time, but on a scale never required before. It's a very old idea that may actually hold the key to a new age of 'global democracy.'"

"NOT A SIGN OF WEAKNESS"

ALF's week in the wilderness moved Claire Spain-Rémy (ALF-Tacoma) to release some outdated notions of who she is:

As a doctor, and particularly as a surgeon, I've never been a big one for process. I lived for results, results that I usually could attribute to something that I had analyzed, diagnosed, and treated. I spent my days accomplishing something every thirty minutes, or maybe every couple of hours. Then I tucked that problem away and went on to the next one.

> "People don't want to follow you because you're perfect. They want to follow you because you're human."
>
> —Pamela Jefsen,
> ALF-Charlotte Region

But here I was challenged to explore the pathway, to learn what being collaborative really meant and why it was important, to be willing to change directions or even not achieve the planned destination. What was this? This was chaos. I have spent my life trying to organize, classify, plan, and achieve and now you want me to "lean in" and see where things take me?

But I did. I opened myself. I studied servant leadership and saw it demonstrated by a big, authoritative man who quietly carried a latrine up a ravine. For the first time in my life I accepted help with something that I could accomplish on my own but could do more easily when someone reached out a hand to help me over a rocky stream. I learned from my foolishness at trying to talk someone up the last leg of the mountain—after all, *I* knew the pinnacle was what was important—when he knew he shouldn't go. I saw a man much my senior make it down from the summit and go right back up to lend encouragement and a gentle guiding hand to someone struggling.

A classmate gave me permission and encouragement to cry—one of the best gifts that I had ever received. With that gift, I was able to say for the first time, "My emotion is not a sign of weakness even if it makes you feel uncomfortable."

Claire Spain-Rémy, MD, is senior vice president for MultiCare Medical Associates and lives in Lakewood, Washington.

"I NEVER KNEW"

As he witnessed the personal stretches that others were willing to make climbing the mountain, Joe Whitworth (ALF-Oregon) decided to create one of his own:

> Within our group of vigorous leaders was a competent professional and respected thinker in her field. She struggled with significant chronic pain. She was hoping to make the climb with us and worked hard during the week to put herself in the physical and mental space to do it. But as the week progressed, so did her difficulties. She ultimately would not make the trip.
>
> Striving both to understand the physical challenges among us and make good on bagging the peak, we split into two groups. Those who were feeling strong would climb the mountain, and the remaining small contingent would set up camp with intentional encumbrances. One classmate duct-taped dumbbells to various appendages and one took no food or water. I chose to put handfuls of gravel in each of my shoes.
>
> From a physical perspective, I have had it pretty good, a lifetime of sports played at high competitive levels. But those rocks lifted a veil of understanding for me. I was immediately reduced to nausea as the sharp objects shifted in my shoes while I gathered firewood and set up the guylines for the tarp. By mid-morning I could hardly tie a simple knot, and by noon I could barely finish my sentences. Things that would normally take seconds to do with my hands now took multiple attempts over many minutes.
>
> I never knew.
>
> A year later I received news that my sister, who had been managing pain from an old accident, was diagnosed with stage four lung cancer. Inoperable. She faced it directly, without medication, in hospice. Resolute courage.
>
> I got home and stayed with her for much of the time before she departed on New Year's Day. Time enough to say everything that needed saying between us. But having that glimpse of the pain, and knowing the relief she must have gained after dealing with it for so long, was key to my dealing with that loss.
>
> I still have those rocks in a jar by my desk.

Joe Whitworth is president of The Freshwater Trust and lives in Portland, Oregon.

GIVING IT AWAY

"I came to ALF ready to do something and I didn't know what it was," says Mel Taylor (ALF-Houston). He began to find the answer in the period of silence during his class' wilderness experience:

> With a new moon rising up above us in the clear Colorado air, I fell into contemplation. A voice came to me on the mountain that said, "Mel, it's your responsibility to give it all away." My life's work and successes and learning and mistakes—it's my obligation to share those with people who want to learn it.
>
> With years of mistakes and successes, all that time of clawing upward and proving ourselves to others, come wisdom and insight. What a shame it would be to leave this planet without giving it all back to those younger and eager-to-serve types who are beginning their journeys and deep dives into leading change. I resolved to be a mentor to others who were interested in what I can offer.
>
> ALF can be a catalyst for so much possibility if we senior fellows continue to give it all away. It is in this way that we get back huge gifts of friendship, connection, trust, and fellowship.
>
> We—I—simply must do this.

Mel Taylor is CEO of The Council on Alcohol and Drugs Houston and lives in Houston, Texas.

AN UNSENT LETTER

"I used to believe that leadership meant getting out in front and pulling the wagon to a destination that the 'leader' chose," says Mike Anderson (ALF-Houston). "All other stakeholders could make cursory suggestions, but should mainly sit and enjoy the ride. The leader got the lion's share of the credit."

When that view changed during Mike's ALF year, so did his ability to climb what had been a difficult professional peak. As administrative judge of the criminal district courts, he was the formal leader of his county's court system. But when it came to his goal of establishing a public defender's office, others around him hadn't been willing to sit and enjoy the ride:

> Our efforts to start a public defender's office had failed for twenty years. There were heels dug in on both sides of the issue. Many of those heels belonged to people on the committee formed to work on the proposal, or their supervisors.
>
> With understandings from ALF in mind, I could feel myself helping to guide the wagon from within the group. Others picked up on the method and used it. We were sticking to the task, engaging in respectful discussion and heading for a common goal.
>
> Then came an opinion column in the Houston *Chronicle*, criticizing all the judges and the entire committee in its effort to create a PD's office. I was furious. All our good work was about to be torpedoed. I decided to respond with a letter to the editor in the same newspaper, defending my colleagues and putting the guest columnist, a public official, in his place.
>
> Draft one of the letter did all that and more just splendidly. It felt very good. Well, pretty good. Or maybe not so great. It was all true and all probably richly deserved, but I realized that if I sent that draft, the game was over. It would likely guarantee the final demise of the Harris County Public Defender's Office.
>
> I spent an entire weekend rewriting, revising, reviewing, and editing that letter. I sent the fifth draft to the paper. It detailed the monumental effort that was under way to succeed. And it honestly invited the columnist to join our efforts, which he did. Twenty of the twenty-two criminal district judges voted to participate and we kicked off the pilot public defender's office with a $4.3 million grant from the state legislature. The office is up and running and getting near-unanimous praise.
>
> The content of that first draft of my response letter grows foggy with time. Thanks to what I absorbed from my ALF experience, it has no significance in the story of the Harris County Public Defender's Office.
>
> **Mike Anderson is the district attorney of Harris County, Texas, and lives in Bellaire, Texas.**

FROM BESIDE AND BEHIND

Cylvia Hayes (ALF-Oregon) says that her service as Oregon's first lady has been enriched by a moment of realization in her ALF year about the variable nature of leadership:

It started with the ALF wilderness week. As an athlete and outdoorswoman, I was not at all nervous about the physical challenges. Rappelling off a cliff didn't bother me. I was comfortable with rock climbing. The ALF trainers had pulled me to the front of the class to demonstrate how to do those things. By day three my classmates were calling me G.I. Jane.

That's when Bill, one of our wonderful trainers, began to talk about leading from beside and behind. I was fascinated. I had never before thought of leadership as anything other than being in front. As the class began planning our trek to the summit, some classmates urged me to lead the hike. I admit being pleased that they recognized and trusted my physical competence. I wanted to take charge.

But I decided to try something new. A few of us donned extra-large backpacks so we could carry belongings of classmates who might need help. I took a place in the middle of the pack. Our pace became glacial and the breaks frequent as the trail steepened. Those of us with large packs began lightening the loads of our weary classmates.

Hours later, with the summit in sight, fear of heights overcame one of my classmates. She refused to go any further along the increasingly narrow ridgeline. "Look," I told her, "you are a strong, tough woman who has come through a lot. You are not going to let your class down and you are not going to let a little pile of rocks beat you!" She got up and inched her way along. With that, every member of our class made it to the summit.

By declining to lead the hike, I allowed space for other classmates to step into the front leadership position. I later learned that one of them very much wanted to do so, but was not speaking up—another important lesson in my work with others ever since.

The truth is that *if I had led from the front, I don't think our entire class would have made it to the summit*. I wouldn't have had the patience to move as slowly as required for all of us to succeed. The woman who led the hike was a part-time nature guide with the necessary patience to support people who were physically challenged or uncomfortable out of doors. It turned out that patience in front was more important to the group's success than physical prowess. My gung-ho attitude was more valuable carrying my classmates' belongings and encouraging those who were trailing.

Now my service as first lady feels something like a doctoral program in leading from beside and behind! After many years working on clean energy and sustainable economic development, I suddenly felt blocked from openly contributing my expertise. I wasn't a state employee or member of the governor's staff, which complicated my participation in certain formal meetings. And even though I wasn't paid for my policy work, the governor's team was concerned about public perception. So my policy development leadership was kept behind the scenes. I was leading from behind.

And the aura associated with high political office is a powerful phenomenon. Even at events in which I am the keynote speaker, the governor becomes the focal point when he appears. Although awkward at times, his appearance and participation is always good for the cause and I love having him there. This is leading from beside. As I grow into this role and strive to make the most of it in service to positive change, I am consciously applying the lessons I learned in ALF.

Cylvia Hayes is founder and CEO of 3EStrategies and first lady of Oregon and lives in Bend and Salem, Oregon.

PART III

LEADERSHIP EVOLVING:
OUR DIALOGUE ON WHAT LIES AHEAD

CHAPTER 9:
EVOLVING COLLABORATION

IF THOSE OF US whose names appear at the beginning of this book were in any danger of forgetting the evolving, adaptive nature of collaborative endeavors, the process of writing together served as a potent reminder.

There's a quiet phrase on the cover that is as important to us as the more conspicuous title; the book was written *in Dialogue with* the five of us—Anne, Chris, Kent, Robin and Sharon—who originally came together to accomplish this project. Those three words are carefully chosen. We are fully dedicated to Dialogue as a means to access the collective wisdom and experience of the group. But that doesn't make it an easy practice. Or more accurately, we find it easy to the degree that we manifest the whole set of values described in these pages.

The project began in early 2010. The ALF National Board of Trustees decided to mark the organization's upcoming thirtieth anniversary with an initiative to collect and share the broad strokes of what had been learned over those years, and where the permanent inquiry into leadership and community change stands today. The centerpiece would be a book that would offer value to senior fellows, practitioners of community change and others who reflect on the art of leadership.

Anne, Chris, Kent, Robin and Sharon set out to begin the work. We identified the areas of focus we wanted to include and divided responsibility for writing the first draft of each, circulating our work for one another's comments and starting to develop a structure that would best integrate them into a whole. Over the months we realized that to produce a well-crafted book in a reasonable period of time, we needed to work with a writer to synthesize, amplify and carry forward our work.

We hired Jeff, an ALF-Oregon senior fellow, to do that, remaining together as an ongoing committee to "participate in the unfolding" of the ALF story into a finished book. Sharon agreed to serve as project manager, attending to the countless details, large and small, required by both book production and collaboration among a group of busy people. Sometime later Erik Hanberg and Mary Holste completed the team with their design and marketing services.

Over the course of a year we gathered in Portland, Oregon numerous times, and devoted many conference calls to the collaboration, with the manuscript-in-progress constantly circulating among us. Coordinating the material we had developed the year before, Jeff shaped the vision and structure of the book in a series of proposals to the group. Some were readily accepted, some revised slightly around the edges, and some were starting points for dialogues that ended with course corrections.

The way was not always easy. None of us are shy about extending our opinions, and intellectual competition is not exactly an unknown impulse for us. The five of us who started the project were deeply invested in its outcome, and at the same time respected Jeff's professionalism and the practical need for him to make countless decisions along the way, decisions that would at times differ from what any one of us might have decided. Jeff respected our initiating role and stake in the project, our dedication to its excellence, and the insights that came from experience with ALF that was more extensive and hands-on than his own.

That ALF had been part of all of our lives gave us a vital advantage. We walked into this collaboration with a set of assumptions that we don't carry into interactions with everyone we meet. We knew that everyone at our table had journeyed up and down more than one mountain, across some rough and unsteady terrain, with their class and in their subsequent work. We knew that none of us were perfect masters of ALF values and practices, or immune to moments of fear, small-mindedness and negative clutter. But our shared ALF experience gave us an important gift: solid confidence that each of us is genuine in our commitment to recognize and learn from those cramped moments, and to keep moving along the path of fully understanding that *the work of positive community change* is not all about us.

So from the outset we gave each other more than the benefit of the doubt. We gave each other admiration, and that was the key to our advantage. We took time for this enterprise, more than some of us thought we had. We listened with more patience and less need to mentally rehearse a counter-point than we sometimes have. When challenged, we assumed that the core intention was no more or less than to produce the best book we could. At one time or another, each of us reflected on the importance of a particular opinion we held: was it vital to our sense of what the book needed, or a more casual preference?

There were rich opportunities to deepen our capacity for collaboration. One involved a lengthy disagreement over whether to include the story of an especially ugly racial slur uttered by one ALF fellow during a class session. There's a story about that incident that we would have liked to have been able to tell, a story of reconciliation and deeper awareness and the intimacy that comes from working out difficult struggles together. But that would have been fiction. What actually happened was that the wound deepened over time and made the experience of that ALF class painfully difficult.

We wanted to detail that story in the book. The work of real people in the world has some deep shadows, and we know ALF's best practices don't always banish them. That acknowledgment, part of a commitment to ongoing growth, would have been evident in this disturbing story.

What was also true for us is that ALF requires an unquestionably safe and confidential container for its class' gatherings. This is an indispensable precondition to developing the trust that underlies extraordinary relationships.

Those were the broad strokes of our dialogue. We talked. We listened. On our own and yet together, we took time to reflect on what we had heard. We edited the passage to strip out any reference to ALF chapter or class or characteristics that could have identified any of those present. With all of that removed, with no apparent way for a reader to identify anyone in the story, we asked ourselves, is there any possibility we were compromising ALF's container of relationship?

Some of us thought there was; if anyone reading the book became an ALF senior fellow, would this story cause her or him the slightest doubt that what was said in the class would stay in the class? In another setting, we might have debated over what is ultimately a subjective judgment about when the container of confidentiality is breached.

With these stakes, we recognized this as a mountain we had to get up together. If any one of us believed that including the identity-free version of the story would compromise a core ALF principle, we would leave it out. And that is, in the end, what more than one of us believed. The story is not in this book.

The resolution satisfied all of us. That's not because we agreed on the substance of the matter, but because the relationship we developed over time sustained and deepened our capacity to listen beyond what happens when we're focused on winning an argument. Our curiosity and concern for what others had to say was rooted in complete certainty that everyone in the room was more focused on ALF's integrity and the quality of our collaborative product than with scoring debate points and carrying the day.

And this Dialogue had an additional side benefit. It focused our thinking on one of the major challenges to leadership we underscore in Part III: despite our best intentions, we have not yet found fully satisfying ways to face the dynamics of racial division. Perhaps that's one of the issues you'll choose to engage in our online dialogue.

We are grateful we had the opportunity to create this book together, and to learn from one another along the way.

CHAPTER 10:
LAUNCHING THE DIALOGUE

THE WIDELY-HELD NOTIONS about leaders during the heyday of Houston's 8F Club and in the wake of Watergate bear little resemblance to what we think today. There's absolutely no reason to believe that the coming decades will alter our current thinking any less, or overturn fewer "certainties," than have the last few.

With that in mind, our attention is drawn to two pivotal questions: how well will the conceptual learnings of Part I and the experiential learnings of Part II weather the changes we know are coming, and probably accelerating? And in an environment of constant change, what is the most intelligent way to build on the foundation laid in the last thirty years by ALF and its senior fellows?

Here we lean on the core values structuring this book, particularly the primacy of relationship and dialogue and collaboration. We invite you, along with those you know who share the impulse to serve the common good, into the relationship of ongoing Dialogue. Here we mean more than the simple, if sometimes elusive, belief that "the we is smarter than the me," more than a technique we choose for the moment to surface good ideas. "Dialogue," we remember from Joseph Jaworski's words, "was not a single circumstance in the [ALF] program, but turned out to be a way of life with the fellows—a way of life to which they became committed."

The online interaction we offer you is different at its core from *debate*, which permeates millions of web pages. While debate can stimulate or inform, our consistent experience is that Dialogue is much more likely to bear valuable fruit. Here again is the useful distinction that Kevin McCarthy, a well-regarded ALF facilitator, offered between the two:

> In a debate, we press our point of view in an effort to prove the rightness of our position and argue against the perspective of others who disagree. We disagree in an effort to strengthen our argument and to persuade others to agree with our original point of view. In Dialogue, diverse perspectives are held together in an effort to explore the complexity of an issue and to discover opportunities for change. In debates we ask: Who is winning? In Dialogue we ask: What am I learning and where can change occur?

We choose to learn with you. We want to know what understanding you've drawn from your experiences in service to the community and the world. We want to know what practices you'll try again and which you won't. We want to know which moments of your community engagement have deeply affected you, and how your internal shifts may have affected your community. We want to see what material you've found—

> "If I had an hour to solve a problem and my life depended on the solution, I would spend the first 55 minutes determining the proper question to ask. For once I know the proper question, I could solve the problem in less than five minutes."
>
> **—Albert Einstein**

in print, audio or video format—that moves you. We want to read the most powerful insight you have today about working with others to create the world you want.

And we very much want to know the *questions* that stir your thinking, because they can be vital fuel for a sustained and robust dialogue. We take to heart Peter Block's observation in *Community*:

> The future is brought into the present when citizens engage each other through questions of possibility, commitment, dissent and gifts. Questions open the door to the future and are

more powerful than answers in that they demand engagement.
…Advice is replaced by curiosity.

Our engagement with ALF, and stories we've heard from senior fellows like those in Part II, point to powerful questions. They are a starting point of our Dialogue with you. In keeping with Dialogue's essential nature, each member of our collaborative group has chosen questions that reflect one of the five values, offering in each case a context to stir reflection and Dialogue.

THE PRIMACY OF RELATIONSHIP

As children, we learn to ride a bicycle with someone we trust supporting us while we figure it out, and releasing us when we're ready. The necessity of trusting relationships doesn't change as we grow older. It is through relationships that people develop the courage to explore possibilities, especially those that entail taking risks.

Ask yourself this: Am I in caring relationships with people who not only "have my back," but are willing to give me a pat on the back when I need it and a shove when necessary? Are there people who know who I am, how many kids and dogs and hobbies I have, what my dreams are, both fulfilled and unfulfilled?

Am I in relationships that matter? If not, you may be creating a closed environment that is perfect for protecting the status quo. The wagons have circled, blocking the way to a future that is distinct from, and not enslaved by, the past.

It is only when our lives are filled with people who matter to us that we can do the courageous work necessary to transform ourselves and the world around us. This is the reason we begin the ALF experience with a seven minute talk that introduces people to one another—not by listing professional accomplishments but by answering powerful questions which get at the heart of our personal stories. This practice is a true and authentic disclosure of who you are and what you care about.

This is also the lesson of the stories we've offered in this book. They show unmistakably how extraordinary work is made possible because people are in deep relationship with one another as a result of their ALF experience.

Our Questions:

- *Are you in relationships that matter?*
- *How can candid personal disclosure—the "seven minute talk," in ALF's culture—change the world?*
- *How can we create a stronger sense that we are all in this together?*
  —from Chris Block, CEO, ALF-Silicon Valley

APPRECIATION, EXPLORATION AND INCLUSION OF DIVERSITY

"This organization does a lot of things well," said an African American woman at a recent ALF conference. "Getting to the heart of the matter on race and diversity issues isn't one of them." As people around her nodded, she described her own class' fumbling attempts to enhance insight and awareness of the dynamics behind racial bias and alienation. After a whole year together, she said, they barely got an inch or two below the surface in their dialogue on interracial understanding.

The experience of different classes on this score varies widely. Some senior fellows credit the intimate companionship of their ALF year with breakthroughs of understanding that were never achieved through intellectual reflection alone; for the first time, they will tell you, they "got" some sense of living with an ever-present undercurrent of discrimination and power disadvantage. But even in some of those cases they might find classmates of color skeptical that this newfound understanding will be durable or transformative. That skepticism has triggered difficult and frustrating impasses in more than one ALF class. There have been times when white senior fellows have wondered out loud what they could do or say to show that they understand the deeply hurtful dynamics of discrimination and race-based disrespect. There have been times—not frequent, but memorable—when their classmates of color have said in response, "Nothing. You can't." For a white

ALF fellow seeking to grow and to embody ALF's core values, that can be difficult and possibly angering to hear.

Examples of this persistent obstacle to profound relationship have taken different forms in different ALF classes. A fellow utters a racial slur, supposedly as a joke, takes no responsibility for the violence of his words, and shatters the class' container of trust and mutual goodwill from that day forward. A Latina native of California is asked in an early class session where she was born, offending her and leaving others wholly puzzled and somewhat resentful that this question would be considered offensive. When a white woman reacts with tearful emotion after an ALF class watches the film of Dr. King's *I Have a Dream* speech, an African American classmate bursts out with anger at the way that outsiders try to appropriate a sacred memory that belongs to *his* culture, generating confusion and hurt that is never fully worked out.

Among all the challenges of understanding and personal connection that ALF fellows willingly undertake, why do racial (and sometimes ethnic) differences stand out as singularly difficult? What is it about this particular dimension of the human experience that can so easily fluster and tongue-tie intelligent men and women who are showing unmistakable progress in their effort to grow and enhance their service to the common good? *Why is it that we're not very good at this?* One senior fellow, a member of both the LGBT and African American communities, offers this perspective:

> Because as class participants we bring lots of strong emotion and political bias around these big issues, in this setting in which we have become emotionally vulnerable, often our hopes and expectations [concerning diversity issues] are higher than what we have the capacity to deliver. In a society in which the dynamics of diversity, equity and cultural competency are very much unresolved, why would we expect that we might create nice neatly wrapped solutions and resolutions in this setting where many people are hearing about concepts of privilege for the first time in their lives (and may not really buy in to them) and others have been immersed in analysis and dialogue

about these dynamics for years. ... The key point is that some chaos and struggle around these issues is very healthy. The perspective that just the right process, curriculum or facilitator will fix the difficulty, challenge and dissatisfaction seems a disservice to witnessing the complexity of the challenges we are being invited to take on in our leadership in the world.

Step one in learning is to first become aware of how little we know and to become aware of our unconsciousness. Only then can we begin the process of developing consciousness and new methods of relating and collaborating.

According to the Kirwan Institute for the Study of Race and Ethnicity, the word "racism" is commonly understood to refer to instances in which one individual intentionally or unintentionally targets others for negative treatment because of their skin color or other group-based physical characteristics. This ignores the fact of structural racism, where racialized outcomes do not require racist actors. It remains a fact that life chances and opportunities in this country are still heavily racialized due to a legacy of institutional bias. This paradox—structural racism without individual racists, where the effects of racism rely more on daily, cumulative acts of omission rather than overt acts of commission—is perhaps the new "transcendent task" of our generation to confront.

Of course, racial difference is not the only rough terrain in the broad landscape of diversity work. Other dimensions have their own particular puzzles, some magnified because the differences at hand are less evident than skin color. Diversity in sexual orientation, for example, is currently generating a vital, robust conversation with its own dynamics. Other layers of diversity—class, gender, age, political orientation —deserve inquiry and collective reflection. We choose to focus on race at this initiatory stage of our Dialogue with you, because that diversity component seems to most frequently generate turmoil and frustration for ALF classes trying to become cohesive and effective teams.

Our Questions:

- *Does leadership have a crucial role in either contributing to racial justice or reinforcing prevailing patterns of racial inequality and exclusion? What examples of this have you observed that we can learn from and incorporate into a broader understanding of the responsibility of contemporary leadership?*

- *What is the role of leadership in a world where intrapersonal racism may be declining, while incidents of structural bias are arguably on the rise?*

- *Current leadership thinking and practice is strongly influenced by values and beliefs that are part of the dominant culture in this country. How can we better understand how this plays out in the leadership of organizations and institutions, and what new paradigms might better serve us in the future?*

—**from Kent Snyder, Chair, ALF Board of Trustees**

DIALOGUE AND COLLABORATION

From the organization's official tagline of *Joining and strengthening leaders to better serve the public good* through the completion of a class project, Dialogue and collaboration are a central connecting thread of the ALF experience. The stories on earlier pages of this book illustrate this value in practice, with resulting achievements that in many cases were beyond the reach of individual efforts, no matter how skilled or determined.

The ALF curriculum offers plenty of opportunity to enhance collaboration skill. We practice Dialogue, consensus, listening, careful inclusion of diverse views. But even when those skills are ably practiced, successful collaboration relies on having adequate *time*. Without that key ingredient—to build trust, to understand different perspectives, to dig deeply enough into a problem to find a solution that best meets the most needs—communities often fail to move the work forward. Our time-starved world, filled to the brim with meetings, emails, RSS feeds, the blaring of 24/7 media cycles, is rarely friendly to the required conditions of full collaboration.

This reality makes some question whether collaboration is possible or even desirable. As the nation becomes more diverse and political stridency continues to push people to take sides, win/lose adversarial approaches have a way of seeming more realistic and compelling. The legal system beckons. Joining advocacy groups and circling the wagons through social media can be comfortable alternatives to the messy task of working together.

Our Questions:

- *In a world where time seems scarce, how do we balance the need for collaboration with the sense of urgency to get things done quickly and efficiently?*

- *How do you "make" time when none seems available?*

- *What, if any, circumstances call for taking a non-collaborative adversarial approach to serving the common good? If there is an appropriate balance between adversarial and collaborative practices in a given situation, how do we find it?*

—from Anne Udall, ALF-Oregon senior fellow and former Director of ALF-Charlotte

SERVICE TO THE COMMON GOOD

One thread that has wound its way through ALF's entire history, from Jaworski's initial reflections through thirty years of study, Dialogue and practical application, is reflection on the nature of what are commonly called leadership traits. In the heyday of Suite 8F, anyone who considered the question might have listed qualities like certainty, assertiveness, persuasiveness, forceful or charismatic physicality, instant decisiveness, cunning and possession of an iron will as the traits of successful leaders.

A list like that seems almost quaint today. The manifest shortcomings of hierarchical and highly individualized leadership have dramatically changed conventional thinking about the qualities that an effective leader brings to the table when working in a diverse community or organizational context. Indeed, ALF's theory of change pushes fellows to question the notion of leadership *traits* altogether.

We have been culturally attuned to the idea of "born leaders," people with extraordinary innate qualities that set them apart from the crowd; while experience and training might expand leadership ability on the margin, natural traits are by definition qualities that each of us either do or (more likely, when it comes to leadership) don't have. Those who sense that they *don't*, in this way of thinking, quite naturally wait for leaders to arrive on the scene, for "somebody" to set things right. This habit of thought may well have been on Peter Block's mind when he wrote in *Community*,

> ...we can stop looking for leadership as though it were scarce or lost, or it had to be trained into us by experts. If our traditional form of leadership has been studied for so long, written about with such admiration, defined by so many, worshipped by so few, and the cause of so much disappointment, maybe doing more of all that is not productive. The search for great leadership is a prime example of how we too often take something that does not work and try harder at it.

As it turns out, neither pole of this argument—that effective community change depends on Natural Born Leaders, or that individual characteristics are utterly unimportant—reflects the experience of ALF senior fellows. Most of them find that personal qualities do in fact play an important role if viewed through a lens focused on service to a broader community agenda. People who embody those qualities can be extremely effective, not in making good things happen on their own, nor in pushing, pulling or persuading others to do what they decide should happen, but in *creating circumstances and interactions* through which good things, as determined and designed by the group, can happen.

Thus understood, the personal qualities of leadership become not innate *traits*, not some special genetic matrix that separates born leaders from the rest of us, but rather a describable mix of behaviors, attitudes and actions that can be cultivated and honed (sometimes with support from programs like ALF) by most people drawn to serving the common good. It is in the orientation of *leadership for the common good* that we find the richest conversations about just what those behaviors, attitudes and actions are—and we invite you to join the conversation.

Our Questions:

- *How do we as leaders help communities, organizations or other groups decide what constitutes the common good?*

- *What leadership capacities are needed in order to engage in effective collaboration and community co-creation?*

- *How do we know when we've done this well? How do we know when we haven't?*

—from Robin Teater, Executive Director, ALF-Oregon

INNER REFLECTION AND PERSONAL GROWTH

At its best, the ALF class year moves people to think about their own lives and relationships and the narratives they've created about themselves and others. Three key program ingredients advancing the value of inner reflection and personal growth are the luxury of time to reflect between class sessions, the discipline of coming back together with a personal check-in each time the group gathers, and the solo that is a part of the wilderness community building experience. Time to reflect, for those willing to take it, can turn out to be more challenging than climbing any peak or rock wall.

I learned there that it is not enough to sit in a room and think on what was not working, how the community could be better, and how my workplace could improve. Somewhere during the ALF year it becomes clear that each person has an opportunity—actually, an obligation—to take responsibility for the effects of his or her own behavior. Peter Block puts us squarely on the hook when he characterizes full engagement in powerful questions as an acknowledgment that we are "guilty of having created this world."

I took from the ALF experience the need to be radically honest with myself. It made me stop fixing and protecting, and start noticing how I feel and what I do, where I hang back, where others come forward, and what kept me in the room when I wanted to leave. Throughout the year I went through stages of offering judgments and opinions and then, with reflection, listening more, learning how to suspend certainty, talking less, and questioning what the group needed from me.

The real learning for me came when class members activated their inner reflection and put their own personal growth into practice. This evidenced honest vulnerability, a respect for others in the room, and clarity about what was and was not the class' business.

Our Questions:

- *How do you contribute to the problem you complain about?*
- *What is the role of personal work and inner development in meeting the civic challenges of the 21st century?*

—from Sharon Babcock, writer and former Executive Director, ALF-Tacoma

Here, then, is the collection of questions we offer to launch the Dialogue:

- *Are you in relationships that matter?*
- *How can candid personal disclosure—the "seven minute talk," in ALF's culture—change the world?*
- *How can we create a stronger sense that we are all in this together?*
- *How do the continued dynamics of race and class in our country help and hinder the work of the common good?*
- *Does leadership have a crucial role in either contributing to racial justice or reinforcing prevailing patterns of racial inequality and exclusion? What are some instructive examples of this?*
- *What is the role of leadership in a world where intrapersonal*

racism may be declining, even while the prevalence of structural bias is arguably on the rise?

- *Current leadership thinking and practice is strongly influenced by values and beliefs that are part of the dominant culture in this country. How can we better understand how this plays out in the leadership of organizations and institutions, and what new paradigms might better serve us in the future?*

- *In a world where time seems scarce, how do we balance the need for collaboration with the sense of urgency to get things done quickly and efficiently?*

- *How do you "make" time when none seems available?*

- *What, if any, circumstances call for taking a non-collaborative adversarial approach to serving the common good? If there is an appropriate balance between adversarial and collaborative practices in a given situation, how do we find it?*

- *How do we as leaders help communities, organizations or other groups decide what constitutes the common good?*

- *What leadership capacities are needed in order to engage in effective collaboration and community co-creation?*

- *How do we know when we've done this well? How do we know when we haven't?*

- *How do you contribute to the problem you complain about?*

- *What is the role of personal work and inner development in meeting the civic challenges of the 21st century?*

Which of these questions stir you? Which call up an experience or insight that can stir us in return? If you appreciate the intention and contributions of people you've read about in this book, then help us understand collectively what won't be discovered individually by posting at www.everythingweknowaboutleadership.org.

We are initiating a process that will have no conclusive end point. It promises no enduring, clear-cut definition of leadership;

even if constant change weren't the nature of civic life, we know that different challenges and ventures call for different dimensions of leadership. "What's daunting," suggests Donna Cole (ALF-Houston), "is that everyone wants a silver bullet. Those that understand know that there is a need for a silver machine gun with hundreds of silver bullets! And it will not be today or tomorrow, but rather years before we can see the significant change."

For all that can't be promised about this Dialogue, those of us choosing to engage with it can look forward to some of the richness of the ALF experience: relationship, collaboration, and the affirmation of knowing that we share our irreducible impulse to serve the common good with many people who may otherwise be very different from us. In this Dialogue you will discover resourceful, generous, inspiring people, realistic idealists who, without comprehensive answers or precise maps, move up the mountain together to do what they can do. Perhaps you are one.

> "I am only one, but still I am one. I cannot do everything, but still I can do something; And because I cannot do everything I will not refuse to do the something that I can do."
>
> —Helen Keller

One more stop before our Dialogue begins: turn the page to see a partial list of some of the most inspiring work for the common good currently underway, complementing but not originating in ALF.

AFTERWORD
LEADERSHIP FLOURISHING: SOME OF THE INSPIRING WORK AROUND US

THE GUIDING VALUES of ALF are not unique to this program. We suspect that many of you are engaged in or know programs that strive toward transformational change. In our local communities, at the state level, and nationally, individuals and programs use the power of relationships, the practice of Dialogue and the commitment to the common good to drive toward powerful outcomes.

All of us engaged in the creation of this book believed it was important to highlight a few examples of national programs around the country that share the values underlying ALF's mission. The information below is taken directly from websites and provides an introduction to the mission and focus. We know this list is only the briefest glimpse of the work around the country and internationally, and invite you to add to it in our online Dialogue. We are eager to build more connections—and hope that this section serves as an invitation to learn from each other.

America Speaks
www.americaspeaks.org

AmericaSpeaks develops innovative deliberative tools that work for both citizens and decision makers. These tools give citizens an opportunity to have a strong voice in public decision making within the increasingly short timeframes required of decision makers. As a result, citizens can impact decisions and those in leadership positions can make more informed, lasting decisions. Since the organization's founding in 1995, AmericaSpeaks methodologies have engaged over 65,000 people in over 50 large-scale forums in all 50 states and the District of Columbia.

....

Association of Leadership Programs
www.alp-leaders.net

ALP's Mission is to provide professional educational activities and to engage, educate, and train leaders. Through recognizing excellence, fostering innovation, sharing best practices, educational training and development, and building networks, we advance the effectiveness of community leadership programs and professionals.

....

CIRCLE Center for Information and Research on Civic Learning and Engagement
www.civicyouth.org

CIRCLE conducts research on civic education in schools, colleges, and community settings and on young Americans' voting and political participation, service, activism, media use, and other forms of civic engagement. It is based at the Jonathan M. Tisch College of Citizenship and Public Service at Tufts University.

Common Bond Institute
www.cbiworld.org

CBI grew out of one of the first Soviet-American non-government human service exchanges initiated in 1982. CBI organizes and sponsors conflict transformation conferences, professional training programs, and relief efforts internationally, and provides needs assessment and resource development, networking and coordination support to assist newly emerging human service and civil society organizations in developing societies.

....

Common Good
www.commongood.org

Common Good is a nonpartisan reform coalition that offers Americans a new way to look at law and government. We propose practical, bold ideas to restore common sense to all three branches of government—legislative, executive and judicial—based on the principles of individual freedom, responsibility and accountability. Common Good's philosophy is based on a simple but powerful idea: People, not rules, make things happen. This idea is fundamental to how we write laws and regulations, structure government agencies and resolve legal disputes. It affects all our lives, every day. Our mission is to overhaul governmental and legal systems to allow people to make sensible choices. We believe Americans need to be liberated to do their best.

....

Community Building Institute
www.communitybuildinginstitute.org

Founded in 2000, the Community Building Institute (CBI) helps public entities, organizations, coalitions, and foundations build inclusive and collaborative processes to make progress on challenging public issues. CBI's expertise in consensus building, strategic thinking and planning, civic engagement, facilitation, and complex process design helps foster the development of agreements that drive transformative change. In addition, CBI works with organizations, creating strategic plans, facilitating boards, fostering staff development, and guiding strategic positioning.

....

Convergence: Center for Policy Resolution
www.convergencepolicy.org

Our goal is to find new ways to solve problems by generating purposeful communications across differences. We are dedicated to forging enduring solutions to important public policy issues.

Our two-part mission is:

- To create wise and durable solutions to major domestic and international challenges confronting the United States, and

- To foment a groundswell in the use of civil, collaborative approaches to national problem solving.

In the short term, our goal is to use our proven method to create policy breakthroughs on national issues caught either in political gridlock or in limbo for failure to pool knowledge across differing perspectives and disciplines. Long-term, our strategic objective is not issue-centric. Rather, it is to generate a tipping point toward the widespread use of civil discourse and cooperative problem-solving approaches at the national, state, and local levels.

....

Deliberative Democracy Consortium
www.deliberative-democracy.net

The mission of the Consortium is to bring together practitioners and researchers to support and foster the nascent, broad-based movement to promote and institutionalize deliberative democracy at all levels of governance in the United States and around the world.

The Democracy Imperative
www.unh.edu/democracy

TDI is a national network of multidisciplinary scholars, campus leaders, and civic leaders in the fields of democratic dialogue, public deliberation, and democracy-building. Our mission is to strengthen public life and democracy in and through higher education. We are a network. Our members share an interest in education for a more deliberative democracy and work together to share ideas; steward and distribute knowledge; develop, validate, and disseminate practices; and encourage innovation. Members contribute resources. Members facilitate smaller communities of practice and help with TDI projects. Members host regional gatherings and get together at TDI-sponsored sessions at national conferences. Members play an active role in reaching out to others to be part of this national movement.

International Association for Public Participation
www.iap2.org

IAP2 is an international association of members who seek to promote and improve the practice of public participation in relation to individuals, governments, institutions, and other entities that affect the public interest in nations throughout the world. IAP2 carries out its mission by organizing and conducting activities to:

- Serve the learning needs of members through events, publications, and communication technology;

- Advocate for public participation throughout the world;

- Promote a results-oriented research agenda and use research to support educational and advocacy goals;

- Provide technical assistance to improve public participation.

Kettering Foundation
www.kettering.org

The Kettering Foundation is an independent, nonpartisan research organization rooted in the American tradition of cooperative research. Everything Kettering researches relates to one central question: what does it take for democracy to work as it should? Or put another way: What does it take for citizens to shape their collective future?

···

Leadership Learning Community
leadershiplearning.org

We strive to advance a more just and equitable society by transforming the way leadership development work is conceived, conducted and evaluated. As part of our core work, we provide members with unparalleled access to resources and networking opportunities. Our members include a diverse group of funders, practitioners and consultants, all of whom are engaged in leadership development work. We identify emerging ideas and methodologies and host face-to-face and online learning opportunities, such as learning circles, where members are invited to explore new developments in the field. We are committed to documenting, posting and publishing the outcomes of the meetings through our pioneering website and wikis.

···

National Civic League
www.ncl.org

Our mission is to strengthen democracy by increasing the capacity of groups and individuals to participate fully in and build healthy and prosperous communities. The core values of the league:

• Faith in people and their unlimited potential to solve problems and strengthen the communities they call home.

- Belief that diversity and inclusiveness are assets to be valued and practiced as a means of moving communities to even higher levels of achievement.

- Conviction that democratic processes are the basis for creating high-performing local governments

....

National Coalition for Dialogue and Deliberation
www.NCDD.org

The National Coalition for Dialogue & Deliberation promotes the use of dialogue, deliberation, and other innovative group processes to help people come together across differences to tackle our most challenging problems. We serve as a gathering place, a resource clearinghouse, a news source, and a facilitative leader for the dialogue and deliberation community and beyond.

....

National Institute for Civil Discourse
nicd.arizona.edu

Established in February 2011 after the tragic shooting in Tucson, Arizona at Congressman Gifford's "meet the people" event, the National Institute for Civil Discourse is a nonpartisan center for advocacy, research, and policy regarding civil discourse consistent with First Amendment principles.

....

National Issues Forums
www.nifi.org

National Issues Forums (NIF) is a network of civic, educational, and other organizations, and individuals, whose common interest is to promote public deliberation in America. It has grown to include thousands of civic clubs, religious organizations, libraries, schools, and many other groups that meet to discuss critical public issues. Forum participants range from teenagers to retirees, prison inmates to community leaders, and literacy students to university students. NIF does not advocate specific solutions or points of view but provides citizens the opportunity to consider a broad range of choices, weigh the pros and cons of those choices, and meet with each other in a public dialogue to identify the concerns they hold in common.

....

NATIONAL POLICY CONSENSUS CENTER
policyconsensus.org

The National Policy Consensus Center (NPCC) is an applied research and development center in collaborative governance that serves both the state of Oregon and a national audience. The Center offers students and faculty real-world experience that informs both research and teaching. NPCC also provides its resources as a credible, neutral forum to leaders and their communities seeking to address public issues and opportunities.

....

PUBLIC AGENDA
www.publicagenda.org

Public Agenda, an innovative public opinion research and public engagement organization, works to strengthen our democracy's capacity to tackle tough public policy issues. Our efforts-online, through PublicAgenda.org, our issue guides and Citizen's Survival Kit, Our Fiscal Future, and on our social networks-and in communities around the country, and through our academic arm, the Center for Advances in Public Engagement, are all focused on ensuring that the public's views are represented in decision-making.

TRANSPARTISAN ALLIANCE

www.transpartisancenter.org

The Transpartisan Center was created for two basic purposes;

- Promote the humanization of the political process, the discovery of common ground by bringing conservatives, liberals, libertarians, progressives and non-aligned leaders together in facilitated dialogues and creating the space for innovative and creative solutions to our pressing challenges to enter into the body politic.

- Promote, support and coordinate transpartisan social and political coalition.

RECOMMENDED READINGS

The following books have been particularly influential in ALF's development and program content:

Better Together: Restoring the American Community, Robert D. Putnam, Lewis Feldstein, and Donald J. Cohen (2004)

Bowling Alone, Robert D. Putnam (2001)

Collaborative Leadership: How Citizens and Civic Leaders Can Make a Difference, David D. Chrislip and Carl E. Larson (1994)

The Collaborative Leadership Fieldbook, David D. Chrislip (2002)

Community: The Structure of Belonging, Peter Block (2009)

Dialogue and the Art of Thinking Together, William Isaacs (1999)

The Fifth Discipline: The Art and Practice of the Learning Organization, Peter M. Senge (revised edition 2008)

The Fifth Discipline Fieldbook: Strategies and Tools for Building a Learning Organization, Peter M. Senge (1994)

Finding Our Way: Leadership for an Uncertain Time, Margaret J. Wheatley (2007)

Healing the Heart of Democracy: The Courage to Create a Politics Worthy of the Human Spirit, Parker J. Palmer (2011)

Knowledge for Action: A Guide to Overcoming Barriers to Organizational Change, Chris Argyris (1993)

Leadership and the New Science: Discovering Order in a Chaotic World, Margaret J. Wheatley (1999)

Leadership on the Line: Staying Alive Through the Dangers of Leading, Ronald A. Heifetz and Marty Linsky (2002)

Leadership Without Easy Answers, Ronald A. Heifetz (1994)

Leadership, James MacGregor Burns (1978)

The Leadership Challenge: How to Make Extraordinary Things Happen in Organizations, James M. Kouzes and Barry Z. Posner (2008)

Old Town New World: Mainstreet and More in the New Economy, Jason Broadwater (2012)

On Becoming a Leader, Warren Bennis (4th edition 2009)

On Dialogue, David Bohm (2nd edition 2004)

On Leadership, John Gardner (1990)

Power and Love: A Theory and Practice of Social Change, Adam Kahane (2010)

Presence: Human Purpose and the Field of the Future, Peter M. Senge, C. Otto Scharmer, Joseph Jaworski and Betty Sue Flowers (2008)

Primal Leadership: Learning to Lead with Emotional Intelligence, Daniel Goleman, Richard E. Boyatzis, and Annie McKee (2004)

The Righteous Mind: Why Good People are Divided by Politics and Religion, Jonathan Haidt (2012)

Salsa, Soul and Spirit: Leadership for a Multicultural Age, Juana Bordas (2012)

The Servant as Leader, Robert Greenleaf (1982)

Solving Tough Problems: An Open Way of Talking, Listening, and Creating New Realities, Adam Kahane (2007)

Source: The Inner Path of Knowledge Creation, Joseph Jaworksi (2012)

Spiral Dynamics: Mastering Values, Leadership and Change, Don Edward Beck and Christopher Cowan (2005)

Theory U: Leading from the Future as it Emerges, C. Otto Scharmer (2009)

Thinking in Systems, Donella H. Meadows (2008)

Turning to One Another: Simple Conversations to Restore Hope to the Future, Margaret J. Wheatley (2009)

The World Café: Shaping Our Futures Through Conversations that Matter, Juanita Brown and David Isaacs (2005)

If other writings have significantly shaped your thinking on leadership and change, please consider mentioning them in our online Dialogue at:

www.everythingweknowaboutleadership.org.

ACKNOWLEDGMENTS

The list of collaborators who helped bring this book to life goes far beyond the six of us.

There are, first of all, thousands of people whose ongoing work gave us *something valuable to write about.* As this book goes to press, the American Leadership Forum is reaching its thirtieth year of effective service because of the dedication of a small number of paid staff and trainers, supported by senior fellows from the program who have donated countless hours as ALF trustees or committee members, or as unofficial ambassadors of the program in the world outside.

Other senior fellows carried ALF principles back to their communities—the stories in this book describe a very small fraction of the whole picture—in ways that fortified ALF's significance and reputation. One of the tangible outcomes of all their activity has been financial support that sustains ALF programs.

We are deeply grateful for that support. It has allowed ALF to develop in alignment with its values. It may be possible to create a leadership program that did not depend on outside donations to sustain itself. But a program determined to bring together leaders from all significant sectors of a community, including those with few discretionary financial resources, cannot succeed without the generosity of individuals, businesses, and foundations that share a vision of diverse networked leadership. Simply and literally, ALF could not have survived as ALF without its committed donors.

Support for the conception and actual writing of this book

came in many forms. The enthusiasm for the project from some of ALF's founding leaders, the encouragement of the ALF Board of Trustees, the considerable logistical support from ALF chapter directors and their support staff, the availability of senior fellows for interviews, and the willingness of some of them to compose stories for Part II on "Leadership Applied" were all vital threads in the finished fabric. A special note of thanks to Andrea Faiss, ALFSV, whose editing work added a great deal to the final product.

We are proud to be your collaborators.

Jeff, Sharon, Chris, Kent, Robin, and Anne

THE AUTHORS

Sharon Babcock

Sharon uses experience from PBS, telecommunications, and higher education in creating innovative partnerships among people in non-profits, industry, government, education, and the media. Sharon is a writer and formerly was executive director of the American Leadership Forum of Tacoma/Pierce County.

Chris Block

Chris is the son of Allen and Marion Block and was born in Los Gatos, California in 1961. He has been involved with ALF-Silicon Valley since he was a member of Class XVI and has been working full time with ALFSV since 2008. Prior to that, Chris spent twenty-five years as an affordable housing developer. Currently he is the ALF-Silicon Valley CEO.

Jeff Golden, principal writer and researcher

Jeff draws from thirty years in politics and public broadcasting to push for an expanded sense of human possibility in his books *Forest Blood, As If We Were Grownups*, and *UNAFRAID: A Novel of the Possible*. He created and hosts the public TV series *Immense Possibilities* and can be contacted for writing services at jeff@immensepossibilites.org.

Kent Snyder

Kent chairs the National Board of Trustees of the American Leadership Forum. After three decades working as a bankruptcy attorney, Kent is now a sustainability consultant and investment advisor in Portland, Oregon. His experience includes service on non-profit and for-profit boards as well as governmental commissions and committees.

Robin Teater

Robin joined the American Leadership Forum of Oregon as executive director in January 2002. Her previous experience spans nearly three decades in non-profit administration, as well as high school teaching in a small rural community in Oregon and as a Peace Corps volunteer in southern Africa.

Anne Udall

Anne has been engaged with the American Leadership Forum for the past 14 years—as the leader of the Charlotte Region Chapter, a national board member and an Oregon senior fellow. She is an educator, facilitator, and leader in the education and non-profit arenas.

INDEX

6197352R00094

Made in the USA
San Bernardino, CA
03 December 2013